GO!

with Microsoft®

Outlook 2013

Getting Started

D0140449

GO!
with Microsoft®

Outlook 2013
Getting Started

Shelley Gaskin and Arkova Scott

PEARSON

Boston   Columbus   Indianapolis   New York   San Francisco   Upper Saddle River
Amsterdam   Cape Town   Dubai   London   Madrid   Milan   Munich   Paris   Montréal   Toronto
Delhi   Mexico City   São Paulo   Sydney   Hong Kong   Seoul   Singapore   Taipei   Tokyo

Editor in Chief: Michael Payne
Executive Acquisitions Editor: Jenifer Niles
Editorial Project Manager: Carly Prakapas
Product Development Manager: Laura Burgess
Development Editor: Cheryl Slavik
Editorial Assistant: Andra Skaalrud
Director of Marketing: Maggie Leen
Marketing Manager: Brad Forrester
Marketing Coordinator: Susan Osterlitz
Managing Editor: Camille Trentacoste
Senior Production Project Manager: Rhonda Aversa
Operations Specialist: Maura Zaldivar-Garcia

Senior Art Director: Jonathan Boylan
Cover Photo: © photobar/Fotolia
Associate Director of Design: Blair Brown
Director of Media Development: Taylor Ragan
Media Project Manager, Production: John Cassar
Full-Service Project Management: PreMediaGlobal
Composition: PreMediaGlobal
Printer/Binder: Webcrafters, Inc.
Cover Printer: Lehigh-Phoenix Color/Hagerstown
Text Font: MinionPro

Credits and acknowledgments borrowed from other sources and reproduced, with permission, in this textbook appear on the appropriate page within text. Microsoft and/or its respective suppliers make no representations about the suitability of the information contained in the documents and related graphics published as part of the services for any purpose. All such documents and related graphics are provided "as is" without warranty of any kind.

Microsoft and/or its respective suppliers hereby disclaim all warranties and conditions with regard to this information, including all warranties and conditions of merchantability, whether express, implied or statutory, fitness for a particular purpose, title and non-infringement. In no event shall Microsoft and/or its respective suppliers be liable for any special, indirect or consequential damages or any damages whatsoever resulting from loss of use, data or profits, whether in an action of contract, negligence or other tortious action, arising out of or in connection with the use or performance of information available from the services.

The documents and related graphics contained herein could include technical inaccuracies or typographical errors. Changes are periodically added to the information herein. Microsoft and/or its respective suppliers may make improvements and/or changes in the product(s) and/or the program(s) described herein at any time.

Microsoft® and Windows® are registered trademarks of the Microsoft Corporation in the U.S.A. and other countries. This book is not sponsored or endorsed by or affiliated with the Microsoft Corporation.

Many of the designations by manufacturers and sellers to distinguish their products are claimed as trademarks. Where those designations appear in this book, and the publisher was aware of a trademark claim, the designations have been printed in initial caps or all caps.

Library of Congress Cataloging-in-Publication Data on File

10 9 8 7 6 5 4 3 2 1

ISBN 10: 0-13-341742-5
ISBN 13: 978-0-13-341742-5

Table of Contents

Chapter 1   Getting Started with Microsoft Outlook 2013 1

PROJECT 1A Inbox 2

Objective 1 Start and Navigate Outlook   3
Activity 1.01   Creating a Local User Account in Windows 8   3
Activity 1.02   Creating an Outlook 2013 Profile   5
Activity 1.03   Exploring Outlook   6

Objective 2 Send and Receive Email   9
Activity 1.04   Configuring Outlook for Sending and Receiving Messages   9
Activity 1.05   Create and Send a New Email Message   10
Activity 1.06   Importing Messages to the Inbox   13
Activity 1.07   Opening, Navigating, and Closing an Email Message   14
Activity 1.08   Opening a Message with an Attachment   15
Activity 1.09   Replying to an Email Message   16
Activity 1.10   Forwarding an Email Message   17
Activity 1.11   Sending a Message with an Attachment   18

Objective 3 Manage Email   20
Activity 1.12   Marking Messages and Formatting Text   20
Activity 1.13   Using the Spelling Checker   22
More Knowledge Checking the Spelling of an Entire Message   22
Activity 1.14   Modifying Message Settings and Delivery Options   23
Activity 1.15   Sorting Inbox Messages   23
More Knowledge Resizing Inbox Column Widths   24
More Knowledge Managing Conversations   25
Activity 1.16   Printing Messages   25
Activity 1.17   Deleting Messages   28
Activity 1.18   Using Outlook Help and Restoring Outlook Email Defaults   29

PROJECT 1B Manage Contacts, Tasks, and Appointments 30

Objective 4 Create and Edit Contacts   31
Activity 1.19   Importing Contacts into Your People Module   31
Activity 1.20   Creating Contacts   32
Activity 1.21   Editing and Printing the Contacts List   34

Objective 5 Manage Tasks   36
Activity 1.22   Creating and Printing a To-Do List   36

Objective 6 Manage a Calendar   38
Activity 1.23   Exploring the Calendar   38
Activity 1.24   Scheduling Appointments   40
Activity 1.25   Printing a Calendar   42

Summary, GO! Learn It Online   44

Glossary   46

Mastering Outlook   48

GO! Think   54

Index I-1

About the Authors

Shelley Gaskin, Series Editor, is a professor in the Business and Computer Technology Division at Pasadena City College in Pasadena, California. She holds a bachelor's degree in Business Administration from Robert Morris College (Pennsylvania), a master's degree in Business from Northern Illinois University, and a doctorate in Adult and Community Education from Ball State University (Indiana). Before joining Pasadena City College, she spent 12 years in the computer industry, where she was a systems analyst, sales representative, and director of Customer Education with Unisys Corporation. She also worked for Ernst & Young on the development of large systems applications for their clients. She has written and developed training materials for custom systems applications in both the public and private sector, and has also written and edited numerous computer application textbooks.

This book is dedicated to my students, who inspire me every day.

Arkova Scott is a faculty member in Business Information Technology at Pasadena City College in Pasadena, California, where she teaches a variety of Microsoft applications including Outlook, SharePoint, Office 365 Lync, Excel, and Access. Ms. Scott is also an instructional designer for the college's award-winning tutor training and First-Year Experience programs. She holds an associate degree in business from Pasadena City College, a bachelor's degree in Computer Information Systems from California Polytechnic University-Pomona, and a master's degree in Computer Information and Technology Leadership from California State University-Los Angeles.

This book is dedicated to my students, from whom I learn so much.

Instructor Materials

Student Assignment Tracker – Lists all the assignments for the chapter. Just add the course information, due dates, and points. Providing these to students ensures they will know what is due and when.

Scripted Lectures – A script to guide your classroom lecture of each chapter.

PowerPoint Lectures – PowerPoint presentations for each chapter.

Prepared Exams – Exams for each chapter.

Test Bank – Includes a variety of test questions for each chapter.

Companion Website – Online content such as the Online Chapter Review, Student Data Files, and Glossary are at www.pearsonhighered.com/go.

Reviewers

GO! Focus Group Participants

Kenneth Mayer	Heald College
Carolyn Borne	Louisiana State University
Toribio Matamoros	Miami Dade College
Lynn Keane	University of South Carolina
Terri Hayes	Broward College
Michelle Carter	Paradise Valley Community College

GO! Reviewers

Abul Sheikh	Abraham Baldwin Agricultural College
John Percy	Atlantic Cape Community College
Janette Hicks	Binghamton University
Shannon Ogden	Black River Technical College
Karen May	Blinn College
Susan Fry	Boise State University
Chigurupati Rani	Borough of Manhattan Community College / CUNY
Ellen Glazer	Broward College
Kate LeGrand	Broward College
Mike Puopolo	Bunker Hill Community College
Nicole Lytle-Kosola	California State University, San Bernardino
Nisheeth Agrawal	Calhoun Community College
Pedro Diaz-Gomez	Cameron
Linda Friedel	Central Arizona College
Gregg Smith	Central Community College
Norm Cregger	Central Michigan University
Lisa LaCaria	Central Piedmont Community College
Steve Siedschlag	Chaffey College
Terri Helfand	Chaffey College
Susan Mills	Chambersburg
Mandy Reininger	Chemeketa Community College
Connie Crossley	Cincinnati State Technical and Community College
Marjorie Deutsch	City University of New York - Queensborough Community College
Mary Ann Zlotow	College of DuPage
Christine Bohnsak	College of Lake County
Gertrude Brier	College of Staten Island
Sharon Brown	College of The Albemarle
Terry Rigsby	Columbia College
Vicki Brooks	Columbia College
Donald Hames	Delgado Community College
Kristen King	Eastern Kentucky University
Kathie Richer	Edmonds Community College
Gary Smith	Elmhurst College
Wendi Kappers	Embry-Riddle Aeronautical University
Nancy Woolridge	Fullerton College
Abigail Miller	Gateway Community & Technical College
Deep Ramanayake	Gateway Community & Technical College
Gwen White	Gateway Community & Technical College
Debbie Glinert	Gloria K School
Dana Smith	Golf Academy of America
Mary Locke	Greenville Technical College
Diane Marie Roselli	Harrisburg Area Community College
Linda Arnold	Harrisburg Area Community College - Lebanon
Daniel Schoedel	Harrisburg Area Community College - York Campus
Ken Mayer	Heald College
Xiaodong Qiao	Heald College
Donna Lamprecht	Hopkinsville Community College
Kristen Lancaster	Hopkinsville Community College
Johnny Hurley	Iowa Lakes Community College
Linda Halverson	Iowa Lakes Community College
Sarah Kilgo	Isothermal Community College
Chris DeGeare	Jefferson College
David McNair	Jefferson College
Diane Santurri	Johnson & Wales University
Roland Sparks	Johnson & Wales University
Ram Raghuraman	Joliet Junior College
Eduardo Suniga	Lansing Community College
Kenneth A. Hyatt	Lone Star College - Kingwood
Glenn Gray	Lone Star College - North Harris
Gene Carbonaro	Long Beach City College
Betty Pearman	Los Medanos College
Diane Kosharek	Madison College
Peter Meggison	Massasoit Community College
George Gabb	Miami Dade College
Lennie Alice Cooper	Miami Dade College
Richard Mabjish	Miami Dade College
Victor Giol	Miami Dade College
John Meir	Midlands Technical College
Greg Pauley	Moberly Area Community College
Catherine Glod	Mohawk Valley Community College
Robert Huyck	Mohawk Valley Community College
Kevin Engellant	Montana Western
Philip Lee	Nashville State Community College
Ruth Neal	Navarro College
Sharron Jordan	Navarro College
Richard Dale	New Mexico State University
Lori Townsend	Niagara County Community College
Judson Curry	North Park University
Mary Zegarski	Northampton Community College
Neal Stenlund	Northern Virginia Community College
Michael Goeken	Northwest Vista College
Mary Beth Tarver	Northwestern State University
Amy Rutledge	Oakland University
Marcia Braddock	Okefenokee Technical College
Richard Stocke	Oklahoma State University - OKC
Jane Stam	Onondaga Community College
Mike Michaelson	Palomar College
Kungwen (Dave) Chu	Purdue University Calumet
Wendy Ford	City University of New York - Queensborough Community College
Lewis Hall	Riverside City College
Karen Acree	San Juan College
Tim Ellis	Schoolcraft College
Dan Combellick	Scottsdale Community College
Pat Serrano	Scottsdale Community College
Rose Hendrickson	Sheridan College
Kit Carson	South Georgia State College
Rebecca Futch	South Georgia State College
Brad Hagy	Southern Illinois University Carbondale
Mimi Spain	Southern Maine Community College
David Parker	Southern Oregon University
Madeline Baugher	Southwestern Oklahoma State University
Brian Holbert	St. Johns River State College
Bunny Howard	St. Johns River State College
Stephanie Cook	State College of Florida
Sharon Wavle	Tompkins Cortland Community College
George Fiori	Tri-County Technical College
Steve St. John	Tulsa Community College
Karen Thessing	University of Central Arkansas
Richard McMahon	University of Houston-Downtown
Shohreh Hashemi	University of Houston-Downtown
Donna Petty	Wallace Community College
Julia Bell	Walters State Community College
Ruby Kowaney	West Los Angeles College
Casey Thompson	Wiregrass Georgia Technical College
DeAnnia Clements	Wiregrass Georgia Technical College

Getting Started with Microsoft Outlook 2013

PROJECT 1A
OUTCOMES
Read and respond to email using Outlook 2013.

OBJECTIVES
1. Start and Navigate Outlook
2. Send and Receive Email
3. Manage Email

PROJECT 1B
OUTCOMES
Create a contacts list and manage your personal information.

OBJECTIVES
4. Create and Edit Contacts
5. Manage Tasks
6. Manage a Calendar

Nmedia/Fotolia

In This Chapter

Success on the job depends on communicating with others and managing your time. Outlook is the tool to help you do those two things. One of the most common uses of the personal computer is to send and receive email messages. Email is a convenient way to communicate with coworkers, business contacts, friends, and family members. Outlook combines all the features of a personal information manager with email capabilities that you can use with other programs within Microsoft Office. Outlook's email features enable you to send, receive, and forward email messages. You can also personalize and prioritize sent and received messages.

The projects in this chapter relate to **Lake Michigan City College** and the **City of Desert Park, Arizona**. The communications within these two organizations will enable you to become familiar with Outlook and practice using Outlook's email capabilities. After you have started using email on a regular basis, you will need to manage your email by deleting messages you no longer need, sorting your messages, and performing other tasks that will keep your Inbox organized. You will practice sending and replying to email messages, and also managing, and printing email messages. You will also use Outlook's Calendar and Tasks.

PROJECT ACTIVITIES

In Activities 1.01 through 1.18, you will start Microsoft Office Outlook 2013 and become familiar with the parts of Outlook. Then you will compose, send, read, and respond to email messages for Darron Jacobsen, Vice President of Administrative Affairs at Lake Michigan City College. You will use various Outlook options and manage his Inbox. The messages you send, reply to, and forward will be stored in your Drafts folder rather than being sent to actual recipients. You will also print a forwarded message. Upon completion, your Inbox, Outbox, and one of the printed messages will look similar to the ones shown in Figure 1.1.

PROJECT FILES

For Project 1A, you will need the following files:

o01A_College_Inbox
o01A_Proposed_Schedule

You will save your files as:

Lastname_Firstname_1A_College_Inbox
Lastname_Firstname_1A_Draft

PROJECT RESULTS

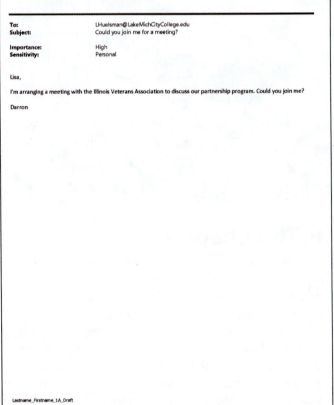

FIGURE 1.1 Project 1A Inbox

Objective 1   Start and Navigate Outlook

Microsoft Office Outlook 2013 has two functions: It is an email program, and it is a *personal information manager*. Among other things, a personal information manager enables you to store information about your contacts in electronic form. *Contacts* are the names of your friends, family members, coworkers, customers, suppliers, or other individuals with whom you communicate. By using a personal information manager, you can also keep track of your daily schedule, tasks to complete, and other information. Thus, Outlook's major parts include Mail for email and Calendar, Contacts, and Tasks for personal information management.

Your email and personal information in Outlook is stored in folders, and there are separate folders for each of Outlook's components. For example, email messages are stored in a folder named *Inbox*. Outlook presents information in *views*, which are ways to look at similar information in different formats and arrangements. Mail, Contacts, Calendar, and Tasks all have different views.

> **ALERT!** **Starting Project 1A**
>
> Because Outlook stores information on the hard drive of the computer at which you are working, it is recommended that you schedule enough time to complete this project in one working session, unless you are working on a computer that is used only by you. Allow approximately one to two hours for Project 1A.

Activity 1.01 | Creating a Local User Account in Windows 8

Do you have or use more than one computer? Perhaps you have a computer at home and also a laptop computer that you use at school or when traveling. Maybe you have, or are thinking about getting, a tablet computer. The frustration of working on multiple computers is that they do not look the same. Settings and favorite websites that you have on one PC do not automatically appear on other PCs that you use. Additionally, if you get a new PC, you must try to set it up all over again to look like your old PC.

With Windows 8, you can create a Microsoft account, and then use that account to sign in to *any* Windows 8 system. Signing in with a Microsoft account is recommended because you can:

- Download apps from the Windows Store.
- Get your online content—email messages, social network updates, updated news—automatically displayed in an app when you sign in.
- Sync settings online to make every Windows 8 computer you use look and feel the same.

To use a Windows 8 computer, you must establish and then sign in with either a local account or a Microsoft account. A new user added to a Windows 8 PC has a choice to sign in with a Microsoft account or a local account.

For purposes of this instruction, it is recommended that you create a *new* local account so that your own email is not intermingled with the projects you will complete in this textbook.

A user account is a collection of information that tells Windows 8 what files and folders the account holder can access, what changes the account holder can make to the computer system, and what the account holder's personal preferences are. Each person accesses his or her user account with a user name and password, and each user has his or her own desktop, files, and folders. Although it is not required that you create a new local Windows 8 user account to complete the activities in this textbook, it is recommended that you do so to ensure that your screens will match the figures in this textbook and so that you do not delete any of your own personal information.

> **ALERT!** Creating a Local Windows 8 Account
>
> It is strongly recommended that you create a new local user account in Windows 8 as described in the following steps to complete this instruction. Doing so will ensure that your own email is not mixed in with this instruction. You can complete this activity if you are logged in as an administrator account, or if you know the administrator password. Some Windows 8 features are available only to users who are logged in with an administrator account; for example, only an administrator can add new user accounts or delete user accounts. If you are logged in with administrator rights, you can complete the steps in this activity. If you are in a classroom or computer lab, check with your instructor for permission to create a new local account.

1 Display the Windows 8 **Start screen**, type **users** and then if necessary, narrow the search to **Settings**.

2 In the list of search results for **Settings**, click **Users** to display the **PC settings**. On the right, scroll down as necessary, and then under **Other users**, click **Add a user**.

3 At the bottom of the screen, click **Sign in without a Microsoft account**. At the bottom of the next displayed screen, click **Local account**.

4 Determine a user name that you will use *only* for this instruction—for example some combination of your first and last name—and then type it as the **User name**. Create an easy-to-remember password, because you may not be able to retrieve it if it is forgotten. Compare your screen with Figure 1.2.

FIGURE 1.2

5 Click **Next**, compare your screen with Figure 1.3, and then click **Finish**.

FIGURE 1.3

6 Point to the top of the screen to display the 🖐 pointer, and then drag down to close **PC settings** and redisplay the **Start screen**. In the upper right corner of the **Start screen**, click the name of the signed-in user, and then click the new user that you just added.

7 Type the password that you created, and then press [Enter]. Wait a few moments while the system creates your local account.

8 When the Windows 8 **Start screen** displays, type **Outlook 2013** to search for the program, and then with Outlook 2013 outlined in white in the search results, press [Enter] to start Outlook on your desktop. Compare your screen with Figure 1.4, which shows the Welcome to Outlook 2013 message.

FIGURE 1.4

Activity 1.02 │ Creating an Outlook 2013 Profile

When you set up Outlook, an Outlook Data File is created for each email account. Additionally, an Outlook *profile* stores information about you and your email accounts. You can connect to more than one email account per profile so that you can manage multiple email accounts within Outlook.

1 With the Welcome message displayed, click **Next**. Under **Do you want to set up Outlook to connect to an email account**, click **No**, and then click **Next**.

2 In the **Cancel Email Account Setup** dialog box, click the **Use Outlook without an email account** check box, as shown in Figure 1.5.

Because you will use fictitious information in this instruction, it is not necessary to connect to a real email account. On your own system, you will want to add your email addresses.

FIGURE 1.5

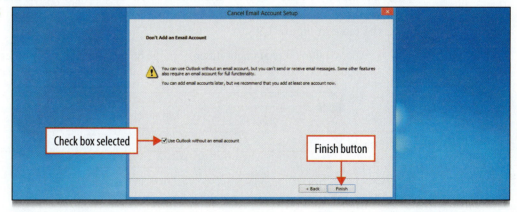

3 Click **Finish**. If a **First things first** message displays, click **Use recommended settings** as shown in Figure 1.6, and then click **Accept**.

FIGURE 1.6

First things first.

○ Use recommended settings
Install important and recommended updates for Office, Windows and other Microsoft software and help improve Office.

○ Install updates only
Install important and recommended updates for Office, Windows and other Microsoft software.

○ Ask me later
Until you decide, your computer might be vulnerable to security threats.

The information sent to Microsoft is to help us and is not used to identify or contact you.
We take your privacy seriously.
Learn more

Accept button → Accept

4 ▶ If necessary, type the administrator password, and then click **Yes**. Compare your screen with Figure 1.7.

> *Outlook Today* is a single screen that summarizes the day's calendar events and scheduled tasks associated with the default email account.

FIGURE 1.7

Outlook Today view

Current date will display

Activity 1.03 | Exploring Outlook

1 ▶ On the left, in the **Folder Pane**, under **Outlook Data File**, click **Inbox**. Compare your screen with Figure 1.8, and then take a moment to study the description of the screen elements in the table in Figure 1.9.

> Your Outlook screen might differ from the one shown. The appearance of the opening screen depends on settings that were established when Outlook was installed on the computer you are using.

FIGURE 1.8

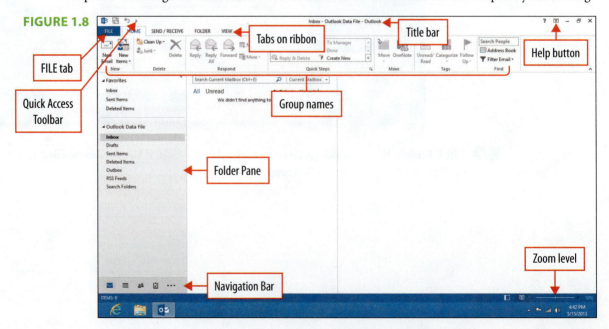

Title bar

Tabs on ribbon

Help button

FILE tab

Quick Access Toolbar

Group names

Folder Pane

Zoom level

Navigation Bar

FIGURE 1.9

MICROSOFT OUTLOOK SCREEN ELEMENTS	
SCREEN ELEMENT	**DESCRIPTION**
Folder Pane	Displays in every Outlook module—Mail, Calendar, People, and Tasks—to display folders related to the module.
Navigation Bar	Displays navigation controls for each of the main views (modules) in Outlook—Mail, Calendar, People, and Tasks—at the bottom of the Outlook window.
Title bar	Displays the name of the program and the program window control buttons—Minimize, Maximize/Restore Down, and Close.
FILE tab	Displays Backstage view, a centralized space for all of your file management tasks such as opening, saving, or printing—all the things you can do *with* a file.
Ribbon	Displays a group of task-oriented tabs that contain the commands, styles, and resources you need to work in Outlook. The look of your ribbon depends on your screen resolution. A high resolution will display more individual items and button names on the ribbon.
Tabs	Display the names of tasks relevant to the open program.
Group names	Indicate the name of the groups of related commands on the displayed tab.
Help button	Displays the Microsoft Outlook Help system.
Quick Access Toolbar	Displays buttons to perform frequently used commands with a single click. The default commands include Send/Receive All Folders and Undo. You can add and delete buttons to customize the Quick Access Toolbar for your convenience.
Zoom level	Displays the Zoom levels on a slider.

2 If necessary, in the upper portion of the **Folder Pane**, to the left of **Favorites**, click ▲ to collapse this group.

3 If necessary, in the **Folder Pane**, click **Inbox**.

The *Mail module* manages your messages and, by default, displays the Folder Pane, Navigation Bar, *message list*, and *Reading Pane*. The message list, located to the right of the Folder Pane in the Mail module, displays your mail messages. On the right side of the screen, the Reading Pane displays where you can preview a message. If your Inbox contains no messages, the Reading Pane is blank.

4 In the **Navigation Bar**, click **Calendar** 🔲, and then compare your screen with Figure 1.10.

The *Calendar module* manages your appointments, meetings, and events. In the Calendar view, the Navigation Bar may display vertically on the left.

FIGURE 1.10

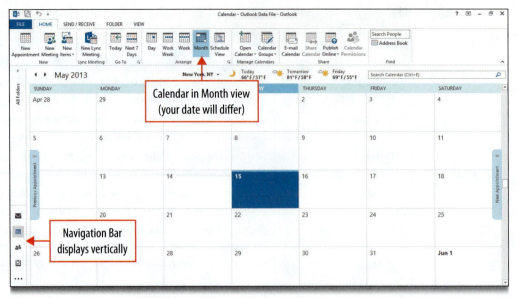

Calendar in Month view (your date will differ)

Navigation Bar displays vertically

5 At the left edge of your screen, in the **Navigation Bar**, click **People** , and then compare your screen with Figure 1.11.

The *People module* manages your contacts—individuals about whom you have information such as their address, email address, phone numbers, and URLs. Depending on whether contacts have been created or imported from other systems, contact names may or may not display in the middle pane of the Outlook window.

FIGURE 1.11

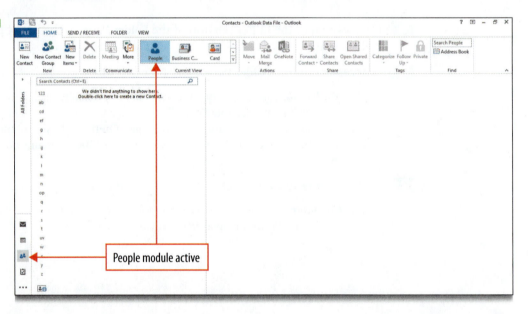

People module active

6 In the **Navigation Bar**, click **Tasks**, and then compare your screen with Figure 1.12.

The *Tasks module* manages tasks, and may display any pending tasks. If no tasks have been created, the list is blank.

FIGURE 1.12

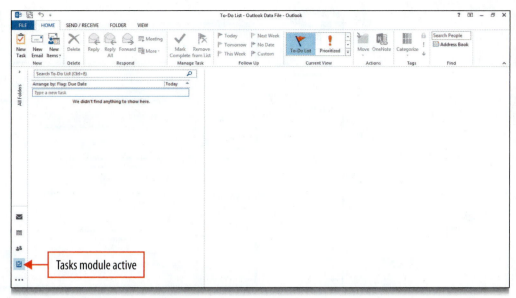

Tasks module active

7 In the **Navigation Bar**, click **Mail** to return to the Inbox.

Objective 2 Send and Receive Email

To send an email message to someone, you must know the recipient's email address. There are two parts to an email address, with each part separated by this symbol @, which is called the *at sign*. The first part is the user name of the recipient. The second part of the email address is the *domain name*. A domain name is the host name of the recipient's mail server; for example, Microsoft's **outlook.com** or Google's **gmail.com**.

Activity 1.04 | Configuring Outlook for Sending and Receiving Messages

If your computer is connected and *online*—connected to your organization's network or to the Internet—Outlook's default setting is to send messages immediately when you click the Send button in the Message form. Copies of sent messages are then stored in the Sent Items folder. If you are *offline*—not connected to a network or to the Internet—messages are stored in the Outbox.

1 Click the **FILE tab** to display **Backstage** view, and then click **Options**. In the **Outlook Options** dialog box, on the left, click **Advanced**.

2 Scroll down to the section **Send and receive**, click to *clear* the check mark from the **Send immediately when connected** check box, and then compare your screen with Figure 1.13.

FIGURE 1.13

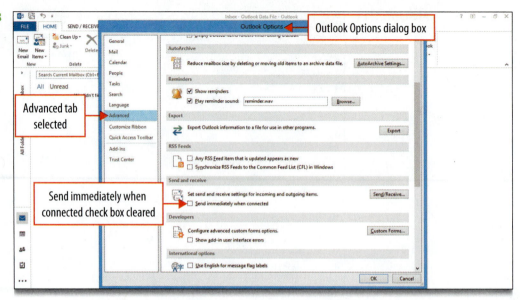

Outlook Options dialog box

Advanced tab selected

Send immediately when connected check box cleared

3 To the right, click the **Send/Receive** button.

4 In the **Send/Receive Groups** dialog box, under **Setting for group "All Accounts"**, click to *clear* the **Include this group in send/receive (F9)** check box, and then click to *clear* the **Schedule an automatic send/receive every** check box.

5 Under **When Outlook is Offline**, click to *clear* the **Include this group in send/receive (F9)** check box.

6 Click the **Close** button, and then in the **Outlook Options** dialog box, click **OK** to close the dialog box.

Typically you would not change these settings; here you are doing so only for instructional purposes.

Activity 1.05 | Create and Send a New Email Message

You can use two editors—programs with which you can create or make changes to existing files—to create and view messages in Outlook. These are the Outlook editor and the Microsoft Word editor. The default email editor is the Microsoft Word editor, with which you can use many Word features when creating your messages; for example, the spelling checker, tables, and bullets and numbering. In this activity, you will create a message for Darron Jacobsen using the Word editor and send it to one of his colleagues at Lake Michigan City College.

1 If necessary, at the top of the **Folder Pane**, click > to expand the pane. Click **Inbox**. On the **HOME tab**, in the **New group**, click **New Email**, and then compare your screen with Figure 1.14.

The top of the form displays a ribbon with commands organized by groups on different tabs.

FIGURE 1.14

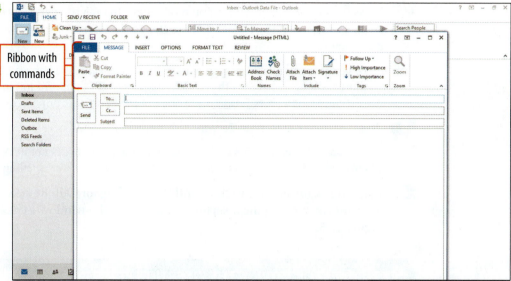

2 In the **To** box, type **LHuelsman@LakeMichCityCollege.edu**

This is the email address of the recipient. Notice the *syntax*—the way in which the parts of the email address are put together. The user name is to the left of the @ symbol, and the domain name is on the right. If another student has used the computer at which you are working, you may see Ms. Huelsman's email address display in blue.

3 In the **Cc** box, click to place the insertion point, and then type **HSabaj@LakeMichCityCollege.edu**

This sends a *courtesy copy*, or *carbon copy*, of the message to the address specified in the Cc box. In both the To and the Cc boxes, you can enter multiple addresses, separating each address with a semicolon. Send a courtesy copy to others who need to see the message.

4 In the **Subject** box, type **Chamber of Commerce presentation** and then click to place the insertion point in the message area.

You can move the insertion point from one box to another either by clicking in the box or by pressing Tab.

> **NOTE** | **Underlined Email Addresses**
>
> Outlook may display an underlined email address after you type it in the box. Outlook remembers previously typed addresses, and this change in its appearance shows that this address has been used before, either by you or by a previous user. Your system may also be set to automatically underline all email addresses that use correct syntax.

5 With the insertion point in the message area of the Message form, type **Hi Lisa** and then press Enter two times.

This is the beginning of your message. It is considered good etiquette to address the recipient(s) by name and add an appropriate salutation. Keep your messages short and to the point. It is usually helpful to the recipient if you restrict your message to only one topic. If you have another topic to discuss, send another email message.

6 Type **I just received confirmation from the Chamber of Commerce; they would like to have you speak at their next monthly meeting. Let's arrange a time for us to meet and discuss your presentation. I'd like Henry to meet with us as well.**

7 ▶ Press Enter two times and type **You might want to look at Joyce's presentation from last month when she spoke at the Illinois Special Needs Teachers Conference. Mary has a copy of it, if you don't have one.**

By pressing Enter two times, you will leave a single blank line between paragraphs. Keep paragraphs short and single-spaced with a double space between them. Do not indent the first line of paragraphs, and press Spacebar only one time following the punctuation at the end of a sentence.

8 ▶ Press Enter two times, type **Darron** and then click somewhere in the text of the message.

Darron is flagged with a wavy red line, indicating the word is not in Word's dictionary. Proper names are often not in Word's dictionary; however, this is the correct spelling of Mr. Jacobsen's name.

9 ▶ Point to *Darron* and right-click, and then click **Ignore All**. Review the message to check for errors by moving the insertion point within the window as described in the table in Figure 1.15.

FIGURE 1.15

KEYSTROKES FOR MOVING THE INSERTION POINT IN A MESSAGE	
KEYSTROKES	**RESULT**
Ctrl + End	Moves to the end of the message
Ctrl + Home	Moves to the beginning of the message
End	Moves to the end of the line
Home	Moves to the beginning of the line
↑	Moves up one line
↓	Moves down one line

10 ▶ Press Ctrl + Home to move your insertion point to the beginning of the message, and then compare your screen with Figure 1.16.

FIGURE 1.16

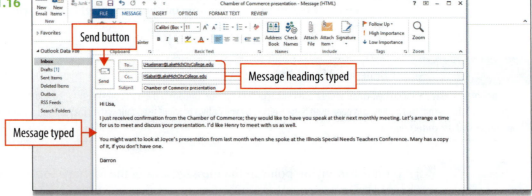

11 ▶ In the message header, to the left of **To**, click **Send**. In the **Microsoft Outlook** message box that displays, click **Add Account**, and then at the bottom of the **Add Account** dialog box, click **Cancel**.

Your message is placed in the Drafts folder. A ***draft*** is a temporary copy of a message that has not yet been sent.

Activity 1.06 | Importing Messages to the Inbox

In this activity, you will import Darron Jacobsen's received messages into your Inbox.

1 In the **Folder Pane**, click **Inbox**.

2 Click the **FILE tab**, and then on the left, click **Open & Export**. Under **Open**, click **Import/Export**, and then compare your screen with Figure 1.17.

The Import and Export Wizard dialog box displays. A *wizard* is a tool that walks you through a process step by step.

FIGURE 1.17

3 In the **Import and Export Wizard** dialog box, under **Choose an action to perform**, click **Import from another program or file**, and then click **Next**.

4 In the **Import a File** dialog box, under **Select file type to import from**, click **Outlook Data File (.pst)**, and then click **Next**. In the displayed **Import Outlook Data File** dialog box, click **Browse**.

5 In the displayed **Open Outlook Data Files** dialog box, navigate to the location where the student files that accompany this textbook are stored. Locate **o01A_College_Inbox**, and click one time to select it. Then, in the lower right corner of the **Open Outlook Data Files** dialog box, click **Open**.

The Open Outlook Data Files dialog box closes, and the path and file name display in the File to import box.

6 Click **Next**. If necessary, to the left of **Personal Folders**, click ▷.

The Import Outlook Data File dialog box displays the folder structure for the file you are going to import.

7 Under **Select the folder to import from**, click **Inbox**, and then click the **Import items into the current folder** option button. Compare your screen with Figure 1.18.

FIGURE 1.18

8 Click **Finish**, and then compare your screen with Figure 1.19.

FIGURE 1.19

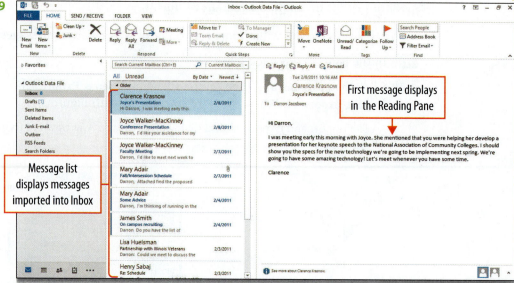

Message list displays messages imported into Inbox

First message displays in the Reading Pane

Activity 1.07 | Opening, Navigating, and Closing an Email Message

You can read messages in two ways. You can read the text of shorter messages in the Reading Pane without opening the message. When the Reading Pane is not displayed or the text of the message is too long to fit in the Reading Pane, you can open the message. In this activity, you will view Darron Jacobsen's messages in several ways.

1 Look at the **Inbox**, and take a moment to study the messages shown.

In the Folder Pane, the number to the right of *Inbox* displays the number of unread messages. In the Mail module, the pane to the right of the Folder Pane is the message list where messages and received items are displayed.

The *message header* for each message includes the summary information about the message such as the Subject, From, and date received. Additional message header details are included in the message's properties.

2 Locate the second message in the **Inbox**, which is from Joyce Walker-MacKinney and has *Conference Presentation* as its subject. Click it one time to display it in the **Reading Pane** on the right.

After you view a message in the Reading Pane, Outlook considers its status as read after you move to another message. The first message indicates that you have read it—the bold blue text is changed to black text.

The Conference presentation message is too long to display entirely in the Reading Pane; however, you can scroll down to view the remainder of the message. Or, you may prefer to open the message to read it.

3 In the **message list**, double-click the **Conference Presentation** message to open it in the message window. Compare your screen with Figure 1.20.

The area above the text of the message contains the message header information, which includes the sender's name and the date of the message. On the left side of the title bar, the Quick Access Toolbar displays, from which you can perform frequently used commands such as saving an item, viewing a previous item, or viewing the next item. In the center of the title bar, the subject of the message appears.

FIGURE 1.20

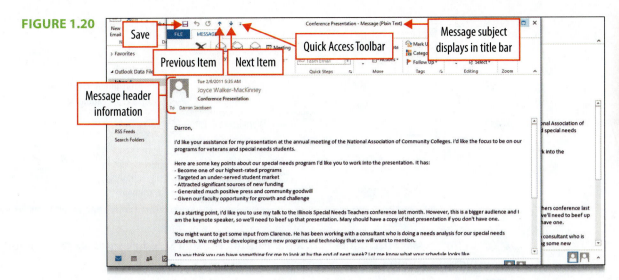

4. In the vertical scroll bar of the message window, click the **down scroll arrow** or drag the scroll box down until the lower portion of the message displays.

5. In the upper right corner of the message window, click **Close** [×].

6. Locate the third message in the **Inbox**, which is the message from Joyce Walker-MacKinney with the subject *Faculty Meeting*, and then double-click the message to open it.

7. In the message window, on the **Quick Access Toolbar**, click the **Previous Item arrow** [↑].

   The message is closed, and the Message form displays the previous message in your Inbox, which is the message from Joyce Walker-MacKinney with the subject *Conference Presentation*.

8. On the **Quick Access Toolbar**, click the **Next Item arrow** [↓].

9. Click the **Next Item arrow** [↓] again.

   The displayed message is closed, and the next message in your Inbox displays. You can view all the messages in your Inbox in the message window by using this toolbar button. When you do so, the current message is closed, and the next message in the list displays.

10. Click the **Next Item arrow** to view the remaining messages in the Inbox. The last message is from Henry Sabaj and has the subject *Alumnus Honored*.

11. **Close** [×] the message window, and notice that no unread items remain in the Inbox.

Activity 1.08 | Opening a Message with an Attachment

A message might include an *attachment*, which is a separate file that is included with the message. Outlook blocks the receipt of files that might contain viruses. For example, any file that has the file name extension of *.bat*, *.vbs*, or *.exe* is blocked. One of the messages Darron has received includes an attachment.

1. In the **Inbox**, locate the message from Mary Adair with the subject *Fall/Intersession Schedule* and click it one time to display it in the **Reading Pane**. Compare your screen with Figure 1.21.

   In the message list, a small paper clip icon displays above the date of the message. This indicates that the message has an attachment. In the Reading Pane, the name of the attachment file displays. The icon representing the Word program indicates that the attachment is a Word document.

FIGURE 1.21

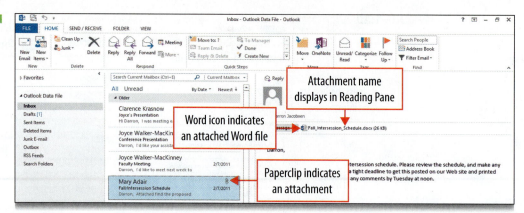

2 In the **message list**, double-click the **Fall/Intersession Schedule** message to open it in the message window.

3 Double-click the **Word icon** in the attachment file name to open the attachment. If necessary, close any Office introductory screens.

4 If Microsoft Word displays the document in Protected View, click **Enable Editing**.

Microsoft Word starts the Word program and displays the attached file, which is a Word document. Note that an attachment is part of an email message unless you save it separately. You can save an attachment separately by right-clicking the Word icon in the attachment file name and then clicking Save As. You will not save this attachment separately.

5 In the upper right corner of the **Microsoft Word** title bar, click **Close** [**x**] to close the attachment, and then **Close** [**x**] the message window.

Activity 1.09 | Replying to an Email Message

You can reply to an email message from the Inbox or while viewing it in the message window. When replying from the Inbox, the Reply button is available on the HOME tab in the Respond group. When viewing the message window, a Reply button is located on the MESSAGE tab in the Respond group. In this activity, you will send a reply to one of the messages that Darron Jacobsen received.

1 In the **Inbox**, select the message from James Smith that has the subject *On campus recruiting* to display it in the **Reading Pane**. Then, on the **HOME tab**, in the **Respond group**, click the **Reply** button. Compare your screen with Figure 1.22.

You do not have to open a message to reply to it—selecting and displaying it in the Reading Pane is sufficient to create a reply. Outlook adds the prefix *RE:* to the subject and title of the message. *RE:* is commonly used to mean *in regard to* or *regarding*. The text of the original message is included in the message area, and Outlook places the sender's email address in the To box.

FIGURE 1.22

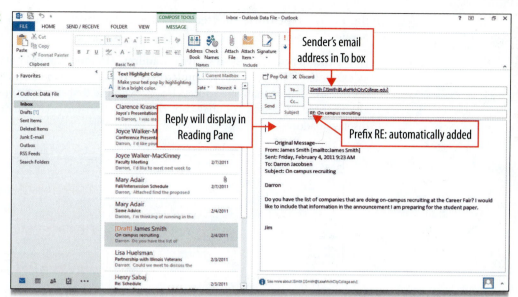

2 With the insertion point at the top of the message area, type **Jim** and press ⟨Enter⟩ two times. Type **I will have the list ready for you by the end of the day**. Press ⟨Enter⟩ two times, and type **Darron**

> A message reply is typed above the original message so that the recipient does not have to scroll down to see your reply.

3 In the upper left corner of the reply, click **Send**, click **Add Account**, and then click **Cancel** to place the message in the **Drafts** folder.

> **More Knowledge** | **Replying to Multiple Recipients**
>
> When you receive a message that has been sent to a group of individuals including you, you can use the Reply All button to send your reply to everyone who received the original message. Be sure that everyone who received the message needs to receive the reply before using the Reply All button. To reply only to the sender of the original message, use the Reply button as you did in this activity.

Activity 1.10 | Forwarding an Email Message

You can forward an email message you receive to someone else—commonly referred to as a *third party*. This is called *forwarding*. However, do not forward messages to others unless you are sure the sender of the original message would approve of forwarding the message. You can forward a message from the Inbox or while viewing the opened message. Darron Jacobsen has received a message that he wants to forward to a third party, Henry Sabaj at Lake Michigan City College.

1 In the **Inbox**, click the Joyce Walker-MacKinney *Faculty Meeting* message to display it in the **Reading Pane**.

2 On the **HOME tab**, in the **Respond group**, click the **Forward** button.

> You do not have to open a message to forward it. On the right, Outlook adds the prefix *FW:* to the subject and title of the message. The text of the original message is included in the message area of the form.

3 In the **To** box, type the first letter of the recipient's address, which is **h** and then compare your screen with Figure 1.23.

Under the To box, Outlook displays the address **HSabaj@LakeMichCityCollege.edu**. This is an example of Outlook's *AutoComplete* feature; Outlook remembers addresses you have typed previously. If more than one address begins with the first character you type, Outlook displays all suggested addresses. You may continue typing the address if you do not want to use any of the displayed addresses.

FIGURE 1.23

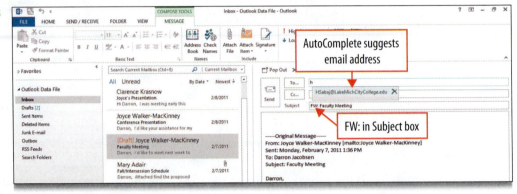

4 Point to *Henry Sabaj's* address and click one time, or, if his address is highlighted, press Enter to accept the suggested address. Then, click to place the insertion point at the top of the message area, type **Henry** and then press Enter two times.

5 Type **As you can see from Joyce's message below, she's asked me to find out if you have any outstanding issues for the next faculty meeting.** Press Enter two times, and type **Let me know.**

6 Press Enter two times and type **Darron** Then click the **Send** button, click **Add Account**, and then click **Cancel** to place the message in the **Drafts** folder.

Activity 1.11 │ Sending a Message with an Attachment

You can attach one or more files to any message you send. When you reply to a message, you may prefer not to include some of, or the entire, previous message. You can delete portions of text by *selecting text* and pressing Delete. Selecting text refers to highlighting areas of the text by dragging with the mouse.

1 In the **message list**, double-click the **Henry Sabaj** *RE: Schedule* message to display it in the message window, and then, on the **MESSAGE tab**, in the **Respond group**, click **Reply**.

2 Click to place the insertion point at the beginning of the second instance of the line *Original Message*. Drag downward to the lower portion of the message area to select the lower portion of the text, as shown in Figure 1.24.

FIGURE 1.24

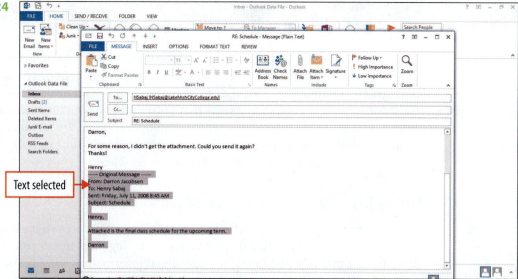

Text selected

3 ▶ Press Delete to delete the selected text. Press Ctrl + Home to place the insertion point at the top of the message area. Type **Henry** and then press Enter two times.

4 ▶ Type **Here it is again**. Press Enter two times, and then type **Darron** On the **MESSAGE tab**, in the **Include group**, click **Attach File**.

The Insert File dialog box displays a list of the drives and folders available on your system.

5 ▶ Navigate to the location where the student files that accompany this textbook are stored. Locate and click the Word file **o01A_Proposed_Schedule**. Then, in the lower right corner of the **Insert File** dialog box, click **Insert**. Compare your screen with Figure 1.25.

The Insert File dialog box closes, and the message redisplays. Outlook attaches the document to the message. The Word icon and the name of the attached file display in the Attached box. If you decide later that you do not want to attach the file to the message, you can click the attachment icon and press Delete.

FIGURE 1.25

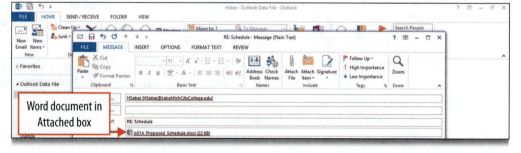

Word document in Attached box

6 ▶ Click **Send**, click **Add account**, and then click **Cancel** to place the message in your **Drafts** folder.

Recall that because this is not a live account, you are placing all outgoing messages in the Drafts folder.

7 ▶ **Close** [**X**] the original message.

Outlook has options that you can apply to messages. For example, you can mark a message to remind yourself or the message recipient to take follow-up action. You can check the spelling of messages you compose. A message can be marked for sensitivity or importance. *Sensitivity* refers to a security label applied to messages that should not be read by others because of the message content—for example, information about employee salaries. *Importance* refers to marks that are applied to messages based on the urgency of the message—for example, information that should be read immediately or information that can be read later.

Activity 1.12 | Marking Messages and Formatting Text

Marking messages as *unread* is one way to draw attention to a message within your message list. Marking a message with a flag—referred to as *flagging*—gives you another way to draw attention to a message and to include additional information with it. You can flag both sent and received messages. *Formatting text* refers to the process of changing the appearance of the text in a message. In this activity, you will reply to one of Darron Jacobsen's received messages, adding a flag and formatting the reply.

1 In the **message list**, select the message from Mary Adair with the subject *Purchase Order*— you might have to scroll down to see this message. Right-click the message, and then click **Mark as Unread** on the shortcut menu.

> Use this command to change a previously read message back to an unread message. A blue bar displays on the left edge and the subject text is blue.

2 In the **message list**, scroll up as necessary, and then double-click to display the Clarence *Krasnow* message with the subject *Joyce's Presentation* in the message window.

3 On the **MESSAGE tab**, in the **Respond group**, click **Reply**. On the **FORMAT TEXT tab**, in the **Format group**, click **HTML**.

> Because the text is in HTML format, you can apply formatting to the text.

4 With the insertion point at the top of the message area, type **Clarence** and then press Enter two times. Type **This sounds like a great idea. Let's meet at 3:00 tomorrow in my office. I will put it on my schedule**. Press Enter two times, and then type **Let me know if this is OK with you**. Press Enter two times, and then type **Darron**

5 Select the sentence *Let me know if this is OK with you*. On the displayed mini toolbar, click **Italic** I to apply italic to the selected text. Click the **Font Size button arrow**, and then click **12** to increase the font size. Click anywhere in the message to cancel the text selection. Compare your screen with Figure 1.26.

FIGURE 1.26

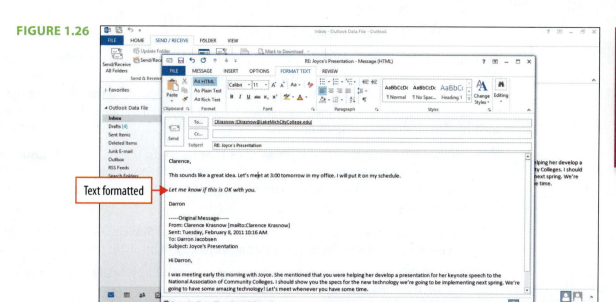

Text formatted

> **6** On the **MESSAGE tab**, in the **Tags group**, click **Follow Up**, and then click **Add Reminder**. Compare your screen with Figure 1.27.

FIGURE 1.27

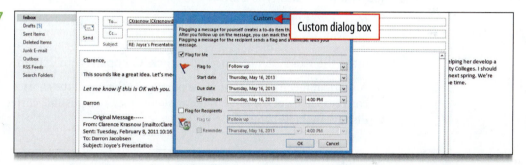

Custom dialog box

> **7** In the **Custom** dialog box, under **Flag for Me**, click the **Flag to: arrow** to view a predefined list of requested actions you can add to the message. From the **Flag to** list, click **Reply**.
>
> You can use any of the predefined messages. Notice that you can also specify a date and time. If the message recipient uses Outlook, a reminder will display on the recipient's system at the appropriate time.

> **8** At the lower portion of the **Custom** dialog box, click **OK**, and then click **Send**. Click **Add Account**, and then click **Cancel** to place the message in your **Drafts** folder. **Close** ☒ the message.

> **9** In the **message list**, select the message from James Smith with the subject *Lunch*. Notice that a red flag displays by the date.
>
> This is how a flagged message appears to you, the recipient. In the Reading Pane, under the message header at the top of the Reading Pane, a banner indicates *Follow up*.

> **10** In the **message list**, click one time to select the message from Joyce Walker-MacKinney with the subject *Conference Presentation*. On the **HOME tab**, in the **Tags group**, click **Follow Up**, and then click the **Tomorrow** flag.

Activity 1.13 | Using the Spelling Checker

Outlook's automatic spelling and grammar checker is active when Outlook is installed. Outlook indicates a misspelled word by underlining it with a wavy red line. To manually check the spelling of a word that has a wavy red line in a message, point to the word and right-click. In this activity, you will send a new message for Darron Jacobsen to one of his colleagues and use the spelling checker to correct spelling errors.

1 On the **HOME tab**, in the **New group**, click **New Email**. In the **To** box, type **LHuelsman@ LakeMichCityCollege.edu** As you type, if the email address displays as a ScreenTip, indicating that Outlook remembers it, you can press Enter to have the AutoComplete feature fill in the address for you.

2 Press Tab two times to move the insertion point to the **Subject** box, and then type **Could you join me for a meeting?** Press Tab one time to place the insertion point in the message area.

> Recall that it is a good email practice to create a subject that is brief and informative for recipients when they view your message in a list of other received messages.

3 In the message area, type **Lisa** and then press Enter two times.

4 Type, but do not correct any spelling errors, as follows: **I'm arranging a meeting with the Illanois Veterans Association to discuss our partnerchip program. Could you join me?** Press Enter two times and type **Darron**

> If you typed *Illanois*, Outlook indicates this word as misspelled by underlining it with a wavy red line. You can also have Outlook find the correct spelling.

5 Point to the word **Illanois** and right-click. Compare your screen with Figure 1.28.

> A shortcut menu displays near the pointer. At the top of the shortcut menu, Outlook suggests a correct spelling of the word. If there is more than one possible correct spelling, the shortcut menu displays multiple choices.

FIGURE 1.28

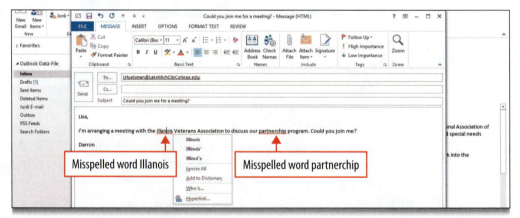

6 On the shortcut menu, click **Illinois** to correct the spelling.

7 Point to the word *partnerchip* and right-click to display the shortcut menu. At the top of the shortcut menu, click **partnership**.

More Knowledge | **Checking the Spelling of an Entire Message**

To check the spelling of the entire message at one time, click the REVIEW tab. In the Proofing group, click the Spelling & Grammar button. The Spelling and Grammar dialog box displays the first misspelled word and displays suggested corrections. You can proceed through the entire message, correcting each misspelled word.

Activity 1.14 | Modifying Message Settings and Delivery Options

Recall that setting message importance and message sensitivity are options that you can use with messages. You can also set various *message delivery options* that are applied at the time a message is delivered. One of the messages you will send for Darron Jacobsen is of a personal nature, and he also wants to know when the recipient has actually read it.

1 With Darron's message to Lisa still displayed, on the **MESSAGE tab**, in the **Tags group**, click the **High Importance** button.

2 On the **OPTIONS tab**, in the **More Options group**, click the **Dialog Box Launcher** button 🔲, and then compare your screen with Figure 1.29.

FIGURE 1.29

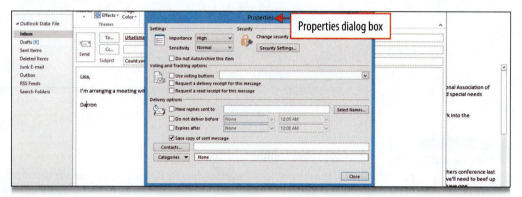

3 In the **Properties** dialog box, notice that under **Settings**, **Importance** is set to **High**. Click the **Sensitivity arrow**, and then click **Personal**.

It is good practice to use discretion when discussing confidential or personal information in your email messages. Recall that the privacy of your email messages cannot be guaranteed.

4 Under **Voting and Tracking options**, click to select the **Request a read receipt for this message** check box.

By selecting this option, you will be notified when the recipient reads this message.

5 In the lower right corner of the **Properties** dialog box, click **Close**, and then **Send** the message. Click **Add Account**, and then click **Cancel** to place the message in your **Drafts** folder.

6 Be sure the **Inbox** folder is selected, and then locate and select the message from Mary Adair with the subject *Purchase Order* to display it in the **Reading Pane**—you may have to scroll down.

When Mary sent this message, she applied the *Importance: High* setting. In the message list, an Importance icon displays above the date, and a banner displays in the Reading Pane.

Activity 1.15 | Sorting Inbox Messages

Sometimes you will want to sort your messages. For example, you may want to see all the messages you received on a specific date or all the messages you received from a specific person. As you will see while working with Darron's Inbox, different arrangements offer a more visually oriented way to work with messages.

1 On the **VIEW tab**, in the **Layout group**, click **Reading Pane**, and then click **Bottom**. Compare your screen with Figure 1.30.

The Reading Pane displays in the lower portion of the Outlook window. When the Reading Pane is turned off or is displayed in the lower portion of the Outlook window, you can see the message *column headings* in the message list. The column headings identify the message *fields*, which are categories of information within an item, such as the subject of a message or the date and time received. Depending upon your Outlook settings, the messages may display differently than the figure. Many Outlook users prefer this arrangement.

FIGURE 1.30

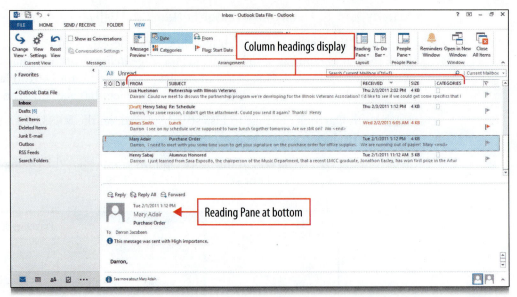

More Knowledge   **Resizing Inbox Column Widths**

When the Reading Pane is displayed in the lower portion of the Outlook screen or is turned off, you can resize the column widths for the Inbox. Point to the divider that separates the message column headers and drag it to the left or right to decrease or increase the width of the column.

2 Point to the column heading **SUBJECT**, and notice the ScreenTip *Sort by: Subject.*

> Use the column headings to sort your messages. The column heading used by default to sort Inbox messages is the *Received* field, with the most recent messages displayed first. The leftmost column headings are icons for sorting by Importance, by Reminder, by Icon, or by Attachment.

3 In the **Inbox**, click the **FROM** column heading, and notice that a pale upward-pointing arrow displays to the right of *FROM*.

> The Inbox messages are sorted alphabetically by the sender's first name. The up arrow in the FROM header indicates that this is ascending order—from A to Z.

4 Click the **FROM** column heading again to change the sort order to descending—from Z to A.

> The downward-pointing arrow in the FROM header indicates that the sort order is descending.

5 Drag the **scroll box** up or down and notice that the messages are grouped by the person they are from.

6 Click the **RECEIVED** column heading to restore sorting by the date and time received.

> Recall that received messages flow into your Inbox by the date and time received, which is the default sort order.

7 On the **VIEW tab**, in the **Arrangement group**, click the **More** button ⏷ and then click **Flag: Due Date**. Scroll to the bottom of the list, and then compare your screen with Figure 1.31.

> The Inbox messages are arranged by due dates, with messages that do not contain a due date displayed at the top of the list.

FIGURE 1.31

Arrangement set to Flag: Due Date

Messages flagged with due dates

8 On the **VIEW tab**, in the **Arrangement group**, click the **More** button ⬇, and then click the **Attachments** button.

> The Inbox messages are arranged so that messages that include an attachment are displayed before those that do not. You may need to scroll up to view the message with an attachment.

9 Click the **RECEIVED** column heading to restore sorting by the date and time received.

10 On the **VIEW tab**, in the **Layout group**, click the **Reading Pane** button, and then click **Right** to display the **Reading Pane** in its default position.

More Knowledge   **Managing Conversations**

A ***conversation*** is a chain of email messages that all have the same subject. If a conversation no longer applies to you, you can click Ignore in the Delete group on the HOME tab. That moves all future messages in the conversation directly to your Deleted folder. On the HOME tab, in the Delete group, click Clean Up Conversation to delete previous messages when a reply includes the earlier message. These features are useful when a conversation includes many recipients and many messages back and forth.

Activity 1.16 | Printing Messages

Recall that Outlook organizes its information in folders. To print information in Outlook, each folder type has one or more predefined print styles associated with it. A ***print style*** is a combination of paper and page settings that determines the way items print. For the Inbox folder, there are two predefined print styles—Table Style and Memo Style. In this activity, you will print Darron's Inbox and Outbox messages in both types of print styles.

1 Be sure your **Inbox** folder is selected so that the contents of the Inbox display in the message list. Scroll up and select the first message in the list—the message with the subject *Joyce's Presentation*. Click the **FILE tab**, and then click **Print**. Under **Settings**, click **Table Style**. On the right, notice the **Preview** image. Compare your screen with Figure 1.32.

> To print a folder list, use the ***Table Style***. Table Style prints selected items or all the items in a list with the visible columns displayed. Use Table Style to print multiple items, such as the contents of the Inbox.

FIGURE 1.32

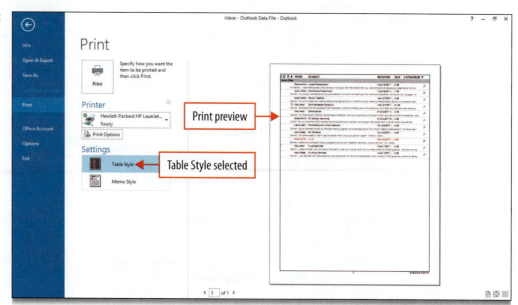

2 Under **Printer**, click the **Print Options** button. In the **Print** dialog box, under **Print style**, click the **Page Setup** button.

3 In the **Page Setup: Table Style** dialog box, click the **Header/Footer tab**. Under **Footer**, click in the first white box to place the insertion point. Delete any existing text. Using your own first and last name, type **Lastname_Firstname_1A_College_Inbox** Do not be concerned if your text wraps to another line. Delete any existing information in the center and right footer boxes. Under **Header**, if necessary, delete any existing text in the three boxes. Compare your screen with Figure 1.33.

Print styles may include the user name, the page number, and the print date in the footer, or they may include other information. If the text you type in the Footer box wraps to two lines, when the page is printed, the footer appears on a single line.

FIGURE 1.33

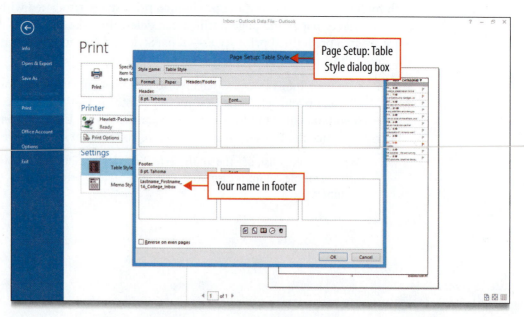

4 In the **Page Setup: Table Style** dialog box, click the **Paper tab**. Under **Orientation**, click **Portrait** if this option is not already selected. Click **OK** to close the dialog box.

Here you can also control the margins and paper size of your documents.

5 At the bottom of the **Print** dialog box, click **Preview**, and notice the footer with your name.

6 To print on paper using the printer attached to your system, click the **Print** button. To create an electronic printout, click the **Printer arrow**, click **Microsoft XPS Document Writer**, and then click the **Print** button. In the **Save Print Output As** dialog box, navigate to your storage location, create a folder named **Outlook Chapter 1** and open the new folder, and then in the **File name** box, using your own name, type **Lastname_Firstname_1A_College_Inbox** and compare your screen with Figure 1.34.

FIGURE 1.34

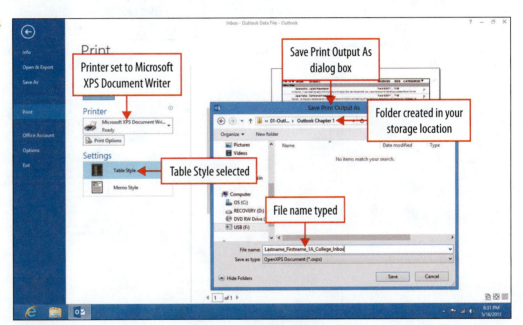

7 Click **Save**, and then submit this file to your instructor as directed.

In Windows 8, you and your instructor can open files of this type—XPS—and also PDF files, with the Windows 8 Reader app.

8 In the **Folder Pane**, click **Drafts** to display the message list for this folder. In the **message list**, click the message with the subject *Could you join me for a meeting?* Click the **FILE tab**, click **Print**, and then be sure **Memo Style** is selected.

Memo Style is the default print setting and prints the text of the selected items one at a time. Use Memo Style to print individual items, such as an entire email message.

9 Using the technique you practiced, add a footer with your name as **Lastname_Firstname_1A_Draft** Delete any other headers or footers, and then **Save** the file as an XPS file in your **Outlook Chapter 1** folder. Submit this file to your instructor as directed.

Activity 1.17 | Deleting Messages

After you read and reply to a message, it is good practice to either delete it or store it in another folder for future reference. Doing so keeps your Inbox clear of messages that you have already handled. When you delete a message in your Inbox folder, Outbox folder, or any other mail folder, it is placed in the Deleted Items folder. Items remain in this folder until you delete them from this folder, at which time they are permanently deleted. You can see that this is helpful in case you delete a message by mistake; you can still retrieve it from the Deleted Items folder until that folder is emptied. You can delete messages in a variety of ways—from the ribbon, from the keyboard, or from a menu.

1 Display your **Inbox** folder, and then select the message from Mary Adair with the subject *Some Advice*.

2 On the **HOME tab**, in the **Delete group**, click the **Delete** button to move the message to the **Deleted Items** folder.

3 Be sure the message from James Smith with the subject *On campus recruiting* is selected. Hold down [Ctrl], and then click the message from James Smith with the subject *Lunch*. Compare your screen with Figure 1.35.

> Use this technique to select non-adjacent (not next to each other) items in any Windows-based program.

FIGURE 1.35

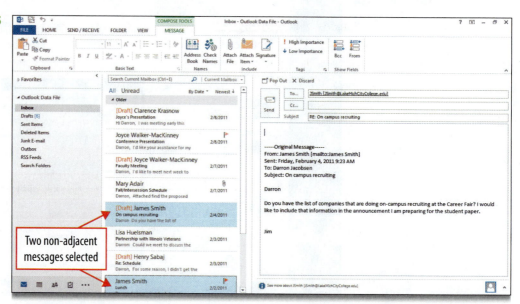

4 On your keyboard, press [Delete] to delete the selected messages.

5 In the **message list**, scroll to the list, click the first message, hold down [Shift], scroll down as necessary, and then click the last message to select the remaining messages.

6 Right-click on any of the selected messages to display a shortcut menu. On the displayed menu, click **Delete**.

> The selected messages are deleted, and the message list for the Inbox is empty.

7 In the **Folder Pane**, click **Drafts**, and then using the technique you just practiced, select all the messages and then delete them.

8 Display the **message list** for the **Deleted Items** folder.

9 In the **Folder Pane**, right-click the **Deleted Items** folder, and then on the shortcut menu click **Empty Folder**.

> Outlook displays a warning box indicating that you are permanently deleting the selected items.

10 In the **Microsoft Outlook** dialog box, click **Yes** to permanently delete the items and empty the folder.

Activity 1.18 | Using Outlook Help and Restoring Outlook Email Defaults

As you work with Outlook, you can get assistance by using the Help feature. You can ask questions, and Outlook Help will provide you with information and step-by-step instructions for performing tasks. In this activity, you will use Outlook Help and restore Outlook's default settings.

1 In the upper right corner of the Outlook window, click the **Help** button [?]. In the **Search box**, type **How do I open an attachment?** and then press (Enter). Compare your screen with Figure 1.36.

> The Outlook Help dialog box displays a list of related Help topics with links in blue text. Clicking these links displays additional information about the topic.

FIGURE 1.36

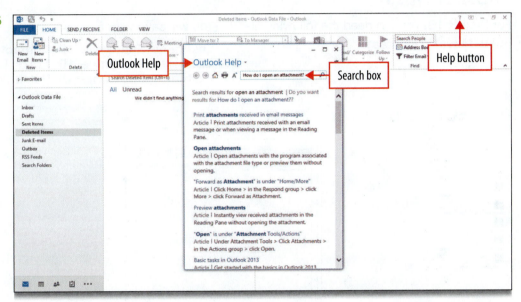

2 On the list of search results, click **Open attachments**, and then review this information.

3 In the **Outlook Help** dialog box, click **Close** [x].

4 Click the **FILE tab**, and then click **Options**.

5 In the **Outlook Options** dialog box, on the left, click **Advanced**. Scroll down as necessary, and then under **Send and receive**, click the **Send immediately when connected** check box. Then, to the right of the check box, click the **Send/Receive** button.

6 In the **Send/Receive Groups** dialog box, under **Setting for group "All Accounts"**, select both the **Include this group in send/receive (F9)** and the **Schedule an automatic send/receive every** check boxes. Under **When Outlook is Offline**, select the check box for **Include this group in send/receive (F9)**. Click **Close** and then click **OK**.

> This action restores Outlook's default settings, which you changed at the beginning of the project for instructional purposes.

7 Click the **FILE tab**, and then click **Exit**. Submit the two files that are the result of this project to your instructor as directed.

END | You have completed Project 1A

PROJECT ACTIVITIES

In Activities 1.19 through 1.25, you will store contact and task information and record appointments in a daily schedule for Shane Washington, Director of Office Operations for Mayor David Parker of Desert Park, Arizona. Upon completion, your Contacts list, To-Do List, and Calendar will look similar to the ones shown in Figure 1.37.

PROJECT FILES

For Project 1B, you will need the following file:

o01B_Mayor's_Contacts

You will save your files as:

Lastname_Firstname_1B_Contacts_List
Lastname_Firstname_1B_Tasks_List
Lastname_Firstname_1B_Calendar

PROJECT RESULTS

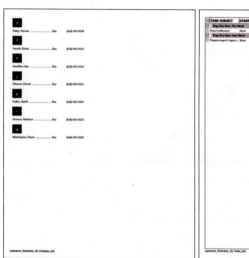

FIGURE 1.37 Project 1B Manage Contacts, Tasks, and Appointments

A **contact** is a person or organization about whom you can save information such as street and email addresses, telephone and fax numbers, birthdays, and pictures. All of your contacts as a group form your address book for storing information about people, organizations, and businesses with whom you communicate. The **People module** in Outlook displays and manages your address book.

Activity 1.19 | Importing Contacts into Your People Module

In this activity, you will **import** contacts into your People module. To import means to bring the information into Outlook from another program in which the information already exists. The imported contacts contain information about various members of the Desert Park city government.

1 Log in to the local Windows account that you have set up for the projects in this textbook, and then start Outlook 2013.

2 Click the **FILE tab**, click **Open & Export**, and then click **Import/Export**. In the displayed **Import and Export Wizard** dialog box, under **Choose an action to perform**, click **Import from another program or file**, and then click **Next**.

3 In the **Import a File** dialog box, under **Select file type to import from**, click **Outlook Data File (.pst)**. Click **Next**.

4 In the **Import Outlook Data File** dialog box, click the **Browse** button. In the **Open Outlook Data Files** dialog box, navigate to the location where the student files for this textbook are stored. Locate **o01B_Mayor's_Contacts**, click one time to select it, and then click **Open**.

5 In the **Import Outlook Data File** dialog box, click **Next**, and then click **Finish**.

6 At the bottom of the **Folder Pane**, in the **Navigation Bar**, click the **People** icon 👥, and then compare your screen with Figure 1.38.

> The first contact on the list—Gloria French—is selected, and her **People Card** displays on the right. The People Card collects all the important details about a contact in one place: phone, email, address, company information, social media updates, and depending on your connection, whether or not the person is available. From the card, you can schedule a meeting, send an instant message, or call the person.

FIGURE 1.38

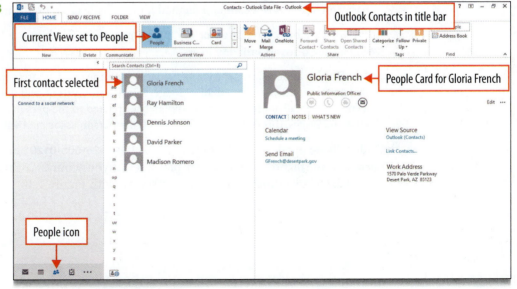

Activity 1.20 | Creating Contacts

When you create a new contact, you add it to your Contacts list. In this activity, you will add Shane Washington, Director of Office Operations for the mayor of Desert Park, as a contact.

1 ▶ In the **Folder Pane**, be sure your **Contacts** folder is displayed. If necessary, click the **People** button on the **Navigation Bar** to display your contacts.

2 ▶ On the **HOME tab**, in the **New group**, click **New Contact**, and then compare your screen with Figure 1.39.

The Untitled – Contact form displays. By using different commands displayed on the ribbon, you can store a variety of information about a person or an organization. A blank area of the form, called the *Notes area*, can be used for any information about the contact that is not otherwise specified in the form.

FIGURE 1.39

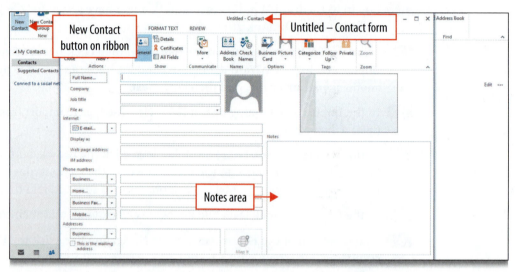

3 ▶ In the **Untitled – Contact** form, in the **Full Name** box, type **Shane Washington** and then press Tab two times.

The insertion point moves to the Job title box, and the form title bar displays *Shane Washington – Contact*. Notice that the *File as* box displays the contact name as *Washington, Shane*. This is how it will appear in the Contacts list. Outlook displays items in the Contacts list in alphabetical order based on last names, a common method for arranging groups of names.

4 ▶ In the **Job title** box, type **Director of Office Operations** Click in the **E-mail** box, and then type **SWashington@desertpark.gov** Press Tab.

The Display as box shows the contact's name with the email address in parentheses. When you use the contact's address in an email message, this is how Outlook will display the address. Sometimes a contact's email address may be completely unrelated to the person's actual name. When viewing email messages, this feature helps you recall the person associated with the email address.

5 ▶ Under **Phone numbers**, in the **Business** box, type **626-555-0129** and then press Tab. If a **Location Information** dialog box displays, select your country or region, type your area code, and click **OK** two times. Compare your screen with Figure 1.40.

FIGURE 1.40

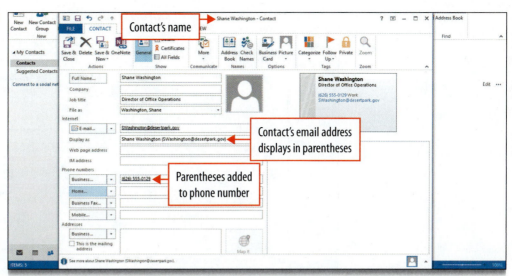

6 Under **Addresses**, click in the **Business** box, and then type **1570 Palo Verde Parkway** Press Enter, and then type **Desert Park, AZ 85123**

7 On the ribbon of the contact form, on the **CONTACT tab**, in the **Actions group**, click **Save & Close**. Compare your screen with Figure 1.41.

> Outlook saves the new contact and the Contacts folder displays. The new contact displays in its correct alphabetical position.

FIGURE 1.41

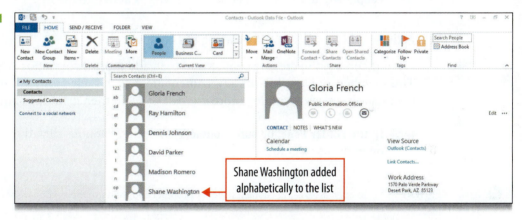

8 In the **Navigation Bar**, click **Mail** ✉, and then in the **Folder Pane**, click **Inbox**.

> The Inbox contains a message from Simone Daley. This message was imported into your Inbox when you imported the contacts. There is no listing in your Contacts for Simone.

9 In the **message list**, point to the text *Simone Daley*, hold down the left mouse button, and then drag the message down so that the pointer is over the **People** icon 👥 in the **Navigation Bar**. Release the left mouse button when you see + attached to the pointer, and then compare your screen with Figure 1.42.

> A contact form displays with Simone's name in the title bar, and the form displays the name and email address of the new contact. If you receive an email message from someone whom you would like to put in your Contacts list, this is a fast way to do so.

FIGURE 1.42

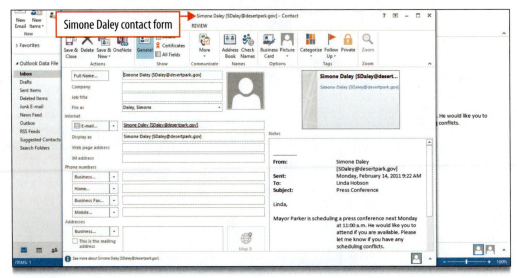

Simone Daley contact form

10 Complete the form by typing the following business contact information:

> **626-555-0128**
>
> **1570 Palo Verde Parkway**
>
> **Desert Park, AZ 85123**

11 On the ribbon of the contact form, click **Save & Close**. On the **Navigation Bar**, click **People** , and notice that Simone Daley is added to the list.

Activity 1.21 | Editing and Printing the Contacts List

It is common to create a contact and then add more information later as it becomes available. Two members of Desert Park's government are new in their positions. In this activity, you will edit the existing entries by adding more information and then print the entire Contacts list.

1 In the **Folder Pane**, be sure **Contacts** is selected. Double-click the **Madison Romero** contact to open the contact form.

> **🔄 ANOTHER WAY**   To open an existing contact, select the contact and then use the keyboard shortcut Ctrl + O.

2 To the left of **Email**, if necessary, click +, and then in the **Email** box, type **MRomero@desertpark.gov** In the lower right corner, click **Save**, and then in the upper right corner, click **Close** **x** .

3 In the **Contacts** list, click **Gloria French** to select the contact. In the **People Card** on the right, at the right edge click **Edit**. To the left of **Phone**, click +, and then click **Work**. In the **Work** box, type **626-555-0123**

4 In the lower right corner, click **Save**, and then compare your screen with Figure 1.43.

FIGURE 1.43

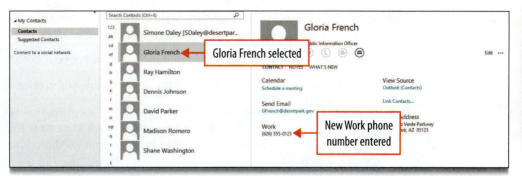

FIGURE 1.43

5 On the ribbon, click the **FILE tab**, and then click **Print**. Under **Settings**, click each setting to see a preview of how the contacts will print.

Each of the different print styles arranges the contact information in a different format. The right pane displays a preview of how the contact information will display when you print it.

6 Under **Settings**, click **Phone Directory Style**.

7 Under **Printer**, click the **Print Options** button. In the **Print** dialog box, under **Print style**, click the **Page Setup** button.

8 In the **Page Setup: Phone Directory Style** dialog box, click the **Header/Footer tab**. Under **Footer**, click in the first white box to place the insertion point. Delete any existing text. Using your own first and last name, type **Lastname_Firstname_1B_Contacts_List** Do not be concerned if your text wraps to another line. Delete any existing information in the center and right footer boxes. Under **Header**, if necessary, delete any existing text in the three boxes. Compare your screen with Figure 1.44.

Print styles may include the user name, the page number, and the print date in the footer, or they may include other information. If the text you type in the Footer box wraps to two lines, when the page is printed, the footer appears on a single line.

ALERT! **Does your screen show a different header or footer?**

Outlook remembers previously entered headers and footers. The boxes for this information in the Page Setup dialog box may indicate a previous user's name or some other information. You can enter new information in these boxes and Outlook will retain this information for the next header or footer you print in this print style.

FIGURE 1.44

9 In the **Page Setup: Phone Directory Style** dialog box, click the **Paper tab**. Under **Orientation**, click **Portrait** if this option is not already selected. Click **OK** to close the dialog box.

Here you can also control the margins and paper size of your documents.

10 At the bottom of the **Print** dialog box, click **Preview**, and notice the footer with your name.

11 To print on paper using the printer attached to your system, click the **Print** button. To create an electronic printout, click the **Printer arrow**, click **Microsoft XPS Document Writer**, and then click the **Print** button. In the **Save Print Output As** dialog box, navigate to your **Outlook Chapter 1** folder that you created in Project 1A, and then in the **File name** box, using your own name, type **Lastname_Firstname_1B_Contacts_List**

12 Click **Save**, and then hold this file until you complete this project.

Objective 5 | Manage Tasks

In Outlook, a *task* is a personal or work-related activity that you want to keep track of until it is complete. For example, writing a report, creating a memo, making a sales call, and organizing a staff meeting are all tasks. Use Outlook's *Tasks module* to display and manage tasks.

Activity 1.22 | Creating and Printing a To-Do List

You can create a new task using a New Task form or enter a new task directly in the To-Do List. In this activity, you will create tasks for Simone Daley, who is the mayor's Chief of Staff.

1 In the **Navigation Bar**, click the **Tasks** icon. On the **HOME tab**, in the **New group**, click **New Task**. In the **Untitled – Task** form, in the **Subject** box, type **Prepare mayor's Japan travel itinerary**

2 In the **Due date** box, click the **Calendar** icon, and then on the displayed calendar, click a date **ten** *business days*—days that are not Saturday, Sunday, or a holiday—from today's date. Compare your screen with Figure 1.45.

FIGURE 1.45

3 On the **TASK tab**, in the **Actions group**, click **Save & Close**, and notice that the **To-Do List** displays the new task.

4 In the **Navigation Bar**, click **Mail**. Locate the message from Simone Daley with the subject *Press Conference*. In the message list, point to the text *Simone Daley*, and then drag the message down to the **Navigation Bar** and over the **Tasks** icon. Release the left mouse button, and then compare your screen with Figure 1.46.

A new Task form opens containing the information in the email. This is a quick way to add a task generated from an email you received.

FIGURE 1.46

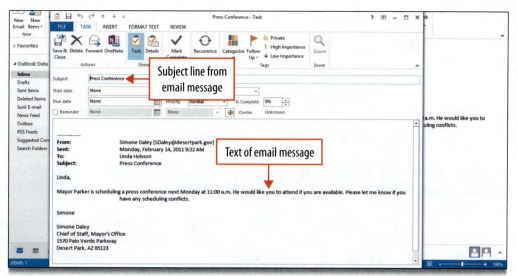

5 Set the **Due date** to the Friday following the current date. Click the **Priority arrow**, and then click **High**. In the *task body*—the area in the lower half of the form—click in the blank area above the email text and type **Complete attendance list for next week's press conference** and then compare your screen with Figure 1.47.

FIGURE 1.47

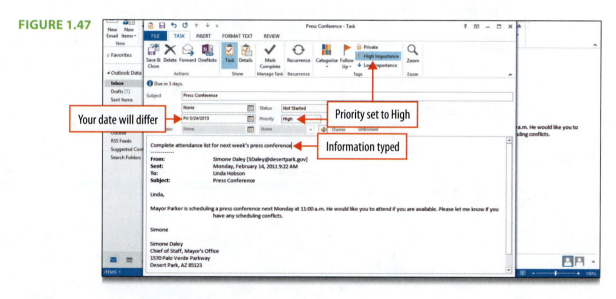

6 In the **Actions group**, click **Save & Close**.

7 On the ribbon, click the **FILE tab**, and then click **Print**. Under **Settings**, click **Table Style**.

8 Under **Printer**, click the **Print Options** button. In the **Print** dialog box, under **Print style**, click the **Page Setup** button.

9 In the **Page Setup: Table Style** dialog box, click the **Header/Footer tab**. Under **Footer**, click in the first white box to place the insertion point. Delete any existing text. Using your own first and last name, type **Lastname_Firstname_1B_Tasks_List** Do not be concerned if your text wraps to another line. Delete any existing information in the center and right footer boxes. Under **Header**, if necessary, delete any existing text in the three boxes.

10 In the **Page Setup: Table Style** dialog box, click the **Paper tab**. Under **Orientation**, click **Portrait** if this option is not already selected. Click **OK** to close the dialog box.

Here you can also control the margins and paper size of your documents.

11 At the bottom of the **Print** dialog box, click **Preview**, and notice the footer with your name.

12 To print on paper using the printer attached to your system, click the **Print** button. To create an electronic printout, click the **Printer arrow**, click **Microsoft XPS Document Writer**, and then click the **Print** button. In the **Save Print Output As** dialog box, navigate to your **Outlook Chapter 1** folder that you created in Project 1A, and then in the **File name** box, using your own name, type **Lastname_Firstname_1B_Tasks_List**

13 Click **Save**, and then hold this file until you complete this project.

Objective 6 | Manage a Calendar

The *Calendar* component of Outlook stores your schedule and calendar-related information. The default location for Outlook's calendar information is the Calendar folder. To add an item to your calendar, display the folder by clicking the Calendar button in the Navigation Bar.

Activity 1.23 | Exploring the Calendar

In this activity, you will use the Folder Pane, Navigation Bar, and the *Date Navigator*—the small calendar displayed in the Folder Pane or in the *Calendar peek* that provides a quick way to display specific dates or ranges of dates in the calendar. Calendar peek is the small calendar that displays when you point to the Calendar icon in the Navigation Bar.

1 In the **Navigation Bar**, click the **Calendar** ▦. On the ribbon, on the **HOME tab**, in the **Arrange group**, click **Day**. Take a moment to study the main parts of the screen. Compare your screen with Figure 1.48.

FIGURE 1.48

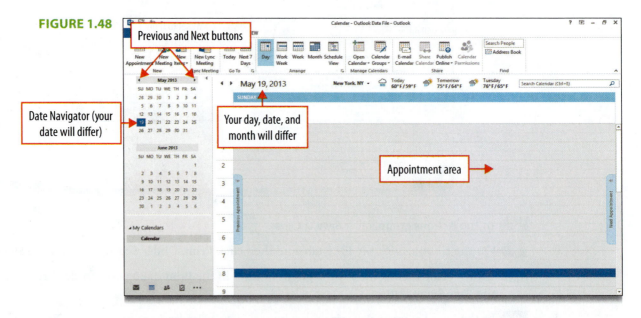

On the right side of the screen is the *appointment area*, a one-day view of the current day's calendar entries. An *appointment* is a calendar activity occurring at a specific time and day that does not require inviting people or reservations. The highlighted date in the Date Navigator and at the top of the appointment area is the date that you are viewing, which is, by default, the current date. On each side of the appointment area the Previous Appointment and Next Appointment buttons enable quick movement to one's previous appointment or next appointment, respectively.

2 In the **Date Navigator**, click a different day of the month.

The date displayed in the appointment area changes to the day of the month you selected in the Date Navigator. In the Date Navigator, the current date remains shaded, and the selected date is highlighted.

3 In the **Date Navigator**, click the **left arrow** next to the month name.

The Date Navigator displays the past month. The appointment area adjusts to the same day in the past month.

4 In the **Date Navigator**, click the **right arrow** several times, moving forward in the calendar two or three months.

The Date Navigator displays future months, and the appointment area adjusts to the same day in the future month.

5 On the **HOME tab**, in the **Arrange group**, click **Week**, and then click **Work Week**.

The *Work Week arrangement* shows only the weekdays, Monday through Friday, instead of the full seven-day week that is displayed in the *Week arrangement*.

6 On the **HOME tab**, in the **Go To group**, click **Today** to return to the current day, and then in the **Arrange group**, click **Day**.

7 Click the **FOLDER tab**. In the **New group**, click **New Calendar**.

8 In the **Create New Folder** dialog box, in the **Name** box, type **Personal Calendar** and then compare your screen with Figure 1.49.

FIGURE 1.49

9 In the **Create New Folder** dialog box, click **OK**.

10 In the **Folder Pane**, under **My Calendars**, click the **Personal Calendar** check box, and then compare your screen with Figure 1.50.

The appointment area splits into two sections, showing both the *Calendar* and the *Personal Calendar* folders. If you use more than one calendar, you can display both at the same time.

FIGURE 1.50

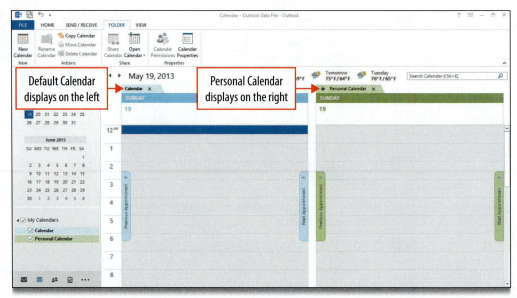

> **11** In the **Folder Pane**, clear the **Calendar** check box to display only the Personal Calendar.

Activity 1.24 | Scheduling Appointments

In Outlook, an appointment occurs at a specific time and day and does not require inviting other people or reserving a room or equipment. You can create a new appointment directly in the calendar by typing it in a blank time slot in the appointment area. In this activity, you will schedule appointments in the Personal Calendar for Simone Daley, who is Chief of Staff for the mayor of Desert Park.

> **1** In the **Date Navigator**, click the **right arrow** one time, advancing the calendar to the next month. Click the **Monday** of the first full week of the displayed month.
>
> The selected date displays at the top of the appointment area.

> **2** In the appointment area, scroll as necessary, and then click the upper portion of the **11 AM** time slot. Type **Weekly meeting with the Mayor** and notice that as you type, the time slot displays green shading surrounded by a black border. Compare your screen with Figure 1.51.

FIGURE 1.51

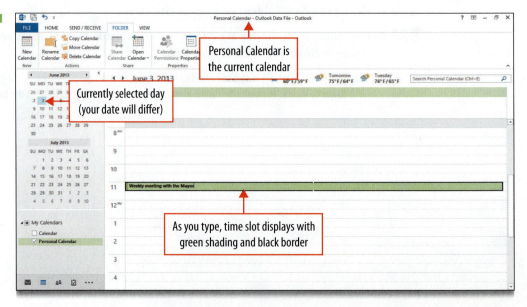

3 Click any other time slot in the appointment area.

> The appointment is scheduled from 11:00 to 11:30. When you use this method to enter an appointment, the default appointment length is 30 minutes.

4 In the appointment area, click the **12:30 PM** time slot—that is, the lower half of the 12 PM time slot—to enter an appointment on the half hour.

5 Type **Lunch with Linda** Click any other time slot in the appointment area, and then compare your screen with Figure 1.52.

> The appointment is scheduled from 12:30 to 1:00.

FIGURE 1.52

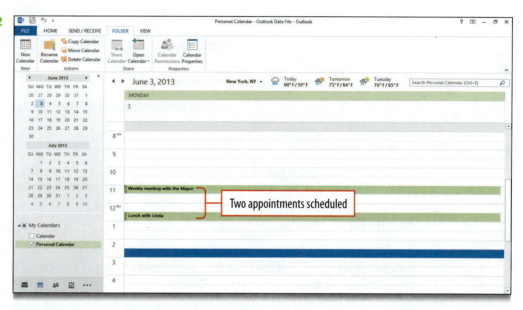

6 On the **HOME tab**, in the **New group**, click **New Appointment**.

> The Untitled – Appointment form displays. You can store a variety of information about an appointment, including its subject, location, starting time, and ending time. Notice that the starting and ending times for the new appointment default to the time you clicked in the appointment area. Space in the lower half of the form enables you to enter information about the appointment not otherwise specified in the form.

7 As the **Subject** of the appointment, type **Meet with Dominique** In the **Location** box, type **My office**

8 In the right **Start time** box, click the **time arrow**, and then locate and click **9:00 AM**. In the right **End time** box, click the **time arrow**, and then locate and click **10:00 AM (1 hour)**.

9 On the **APPOINTMENT tab**, in the **Options group**, click the **Reminder arrow** 🔔 Reminder:, and then click **30 minutes**. Compare your screen with Figure 1.53.

FIGURE 1.53

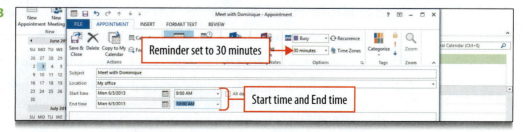

10 ▶ In the **Actions group**, click **Save & Close**, and then compare your screen with Figure 1.54.

The new appointment is added to the calendar. The appointment occupies the 9:00 to 10:00 AM time slot, and the location of the appointment displays below the subject.

FIGURE 1.54

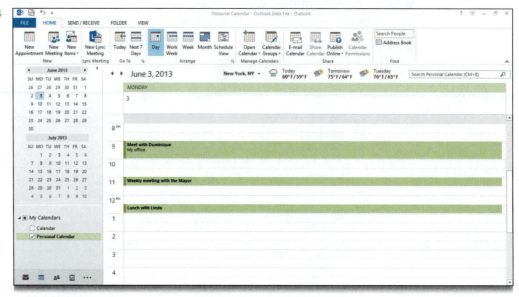

Activity 1.25 | Printing a Calendar

Depending on what you want to print in your calendar, Outlook has a variety of print styles. You can print a range of hours, a day, a week, or a month. You can also print an individual appointment or event.

1 ▶ In the **Date Navigator**, click the **Wednesday** in the week in which you have been entering appointments.

2 ▶ Click the **FILE tab**, click **Print**, and then under **Settings**, click **Weekly Agenda Style**.

Each print style arranges calendar information in a different format. You can preview how the information will display when you print it.

3 ▶ Under **Printer**, click the **Print Options** button. In the **Print** dialog box, under **Print style**, click the **Page Setup** button.

4 ▶ In the **Page Setup: Weekly Agenda Style** dialog box, click the **Header/Footer tab**. Under **Footer**, click in the first white box to place the insertion point. Delete any existing text. Using your own first and last name, type **Lastname_Firstname_1B_Calendar** Do not be concerned if your text wraps to another line. Delete any existing information in the center and right footer boxes. Under **Header**, if necessary, delete any existing text in the three boxes.

5 ▶ In the **Page Setup: Weekly Agenda Style** dialog box, click the **Paper tab**. Under **Orientation**, click **Portrait** if this option is not already selected. Click **OK** to close the dialog box.

Here you can also control the margins and paper size of your documents.

6 ▶ At the bottom of the **Print** dialog box, click **Preview**, and notice the footer with your name.

7 ▶ To print on paper using the printer attached to your system, click the **Print** button. To create an electronic printout, click the **Printer arrow**, click **Microsoft XPS Document Writer**, and then click the **Print** button. In the **Save Print Output As** dialog box, navigate to your **Outlook Chapter 1** folder that you created in Project 1A, then in the **File name** box, using your own name, type **Lastname_Firstname_1B_Calendar**

8 Click **Save**, and then submit the three files you created in this project to your instructor as directed.

9 On the **Navigation Bar**, click the **People** icon ⬛. With the first contact selected—*Simone Daley*—hold down [Ctrl] and press [A] to select all of the contacts. Then on the **HOME tab**, in the **Delete group**, click **Delete**.

10 On the **Navigation Bar**, click the **Tasks** icon ⬛. Press [Ctrl] + [A] to select all of the tasks, and then on the **HOME tab**, in the **Delete group**, click **Delete**. Click **OK** in the displayed message box.

11 On the **Navigation Bar**, click the **Calendar** ⬛ icon. Just above the **Navigation Bar**, point to **Personal Calendar**—be sure you are pointing to **Personal Calendar**—right-click to display a shortcut menu, and then click **Delete Calendar**. When the message *Move "Personal Calendar" to your Deleted Items folder* displays, click **Yes**.

12 Click the **Mail** icon, and then in the **Folder Pane**, right-click your **Deleted Items** folder. Click **Empty Folder**, and then click **Yes**.

13 **Close** ⬛ Outlook.

END | You have completed Project 1B

END OF CHAPTER

SUMMARY

Job success depends on communicating with others and managing your time, and Outlook is the tool to help you do that. Many professionals in business depend on Outlook and use it many times every day.

One of the most common uses of the personal computer is to send and receive email messages. Email is the most frequently used way to communicate with coworkers, business contacts, friends, and family members.

By using the modules Mail, Calendar, People, and Tasks, Outlook combines the features of a personal information manager with email capabilities that you can use with other programs within Microsoft Office.

When you set up Outlook, an Outlook Data File is created for each email account. Your email and personal information is stored in folders, and there are separate folders for each of Outlook's modules.

GO! LEARN IT ONLINE

Review the concepts and key terms in this chapter by completing this online challenge, which you can find at **www.pearsonhighered.com/go**.

Matching and Multiple Choice:
Answer matching and multiple choice questions to test what you learned in this chapter.

GO! FOR JOB SUCCESS

Discussion: Email Etiquette

Your instructor may ask you to think about, or discuss with your classmates, these questions:

FotolEdhar / Fotolia

Question 1: Why do you think it is important to follow specific etiquette when composing an email message?

Question 2: Why is it important to include a greeting and sign every email that you send?

Question 3: What are the differences between sending a business email and a personal email?

END OF CHAPTER

REVIEW AND ASSESSMENT GUIDE FOR OUTLOOK 2013 GETTING STARTED

Your instructor may assign one or more of these projects to help you review the chapter and assess your mastery and understanding of the chapter.

	Review and Assessment Guide for Outlook 2013 Getting Started		
Project	**Apply Skills from These Chapter Objectives**	**Project Type**	**Project Location**
1C	Objectives 1–3 from Project 1A	**1C Mastery** A demonstration of your mastery of the skills in Project 1A with decision making.	On the following pages
1D	Objectives 4–6 from Project 1B	**1D Mastery** A demonstration of your mastery of the skills in Project 1B with decision making.	On the following pages
1E	Combination of Objectives from Projects 1A and 1B	**1E GO! Think** A demonstration of your understanding of the chapter concepts applied in a manner that you would use outside of college. An analytic rubric helps you and your instructor grade the quality of your work by comparing it to the work that an expert in the discipline would create.	On the following pages

GLOSSARY

GLOSSARY OF CHAPTER KEY TERMS

Appointment A calendar activity occurring at a specific time and day that does not require inviting people or reserving rooms or equipment.

Appointment area A one-day view of the day's calendar entries.

At sign @ A symbol used to separate the two parts of an email address.

Attachment A separate file that is included with an email message, such as a Word file, a spreadsheet file, or an image file.

AutoComplete The Outlook feature that assists you in typing addresses by suggesting previously typed addresses based on the first character you type.

Business days Days that are not Saturday, Sunday, or a holiday.

Calendar module A component of Outlook that stores your schedule and calendar-related information.

Calendar peek A small calendar that displays when you point to the Calendar icon in the Navigation Bar.

Carbon copy The term formerly referring to a paper copy made with carbon paper, now used to denote an electronic copy of an email communication.

Column heading Text that identifies message fields.

Contact A person or organization about whom you can save information such as street and email addresses, telephone and fax numbers, birthdays, and pictures.

Conversation A chain of email messages that all have the same subject.

Courtesy copy Represented by the letters Cc, a copy of an email.

Date Navigator A monthly view of the calendar used to display specific days in a month.

Domain name The second part of an email address that identifies the host name of the recipient's mail server.

Draft A temporary copy of a message that has not yet been sent.

Field A category of information within an Outlook item, such as the subject of a message, the date and time received, or a company name or address.

FILE tab Displays Backstage view, a centralized space for all of your file

management tasks such as opening, saving, or printing—all the things you can do *with* a file.

Flagging Marking a message with a flag to draw attention to the message.

Folder Pane Displays in every Outlook module—Mail, Calendar, People, and Tasks—to display folders related to the module.

Formatting text The process of changing the appearance of the text in a message.

Forwarding Sending an email message you have received to someone who did not originally receive it.

Group names Indicate the name of the groups of related commands on the displayed tab.

Help button Displays the Microsoft Outlook Help system.

Import The action of bringing information into Outlook from another program in which the information already exists.

Importance Marks that are applied to messages based on the urgency of the message—for example, information that should be read immediately or information that can be read later.

Inbox The folder that stores incoming mail.

Mail module A component in Outlook that manages your messages.

Memo Style A style that prints the text of the selected items one at a time.

Message delivery options Optional settings for an email message that can include the time a message should be sent or the address that should be used for replies.

Message header The basic information about an email message such as the sender's name, the date sent, and the subject.

Message list Located to the right of the Folder Pane in the Mail module, which displays your mail messages.

Navigation Bar Displays navigation controls for each of the main views (modules) in Outlook—Mail, Calendar, People, and Tasks—at the bottom of the Outlook window.

Notes area A blank area of a form that can be used for any information.

Offline A computer connection status in which the computer is not connected to your organization's network or to the public Internet.

Online A computer connection status in which the computer is connected to your organization's network or to the public Internet.

Outlook Today A single screen that summarizes the day's calendar events and scheduled tasks associated with the default email account.

People Card Collects all the important details about a contact in one place: phone, email, address, company information, social media updates, and depending on your connection, whether or not the person is available. From the card, you can schedule a meeting, send an instant message, or call the person.

People module A component in Outlook that displays and manages your contacts—individuals about whom you have information such as their address, email address, phone numbers, and URLs.

Personal information manager A program that enables you to store information about your contacts in electronic form.

Print style A combination of paper and page settings that determines the way Outlook items print.

Profile The Outlook feature that identifies which email account you use and where the related data is stored.

Quick Access Toolbar Displays buttons to perform frequently used commands with a single click. The default commands include Send/Receive All Folders and Undo. You can add and delete buttons to customize the Quick Access Toolbar for your convenience.

RE A prefix added to a reply that is commonly used to mean in regard to or regarding.

Reading Pane Displays a preview of a message, located on the right side of the screen.

Ribbon Displays a group of task-oriented tabs that contain the commands, styles, and resources you need to work in Outlook. The look of your ribbon depends on your screen resolution. A high resolution will display more individual items and button names on the ribbon.

Selecting text Highlighting areas of text by dragging with the mouse.

Sensitivity A security label applied to messages that should not be read by others because of the message content.

Syntax The way in which the parts of an email address are put together.

Table Style A style that prints multiple items in a list with the visible columns displayed, such as the contents of the Inbox.

Tabs Display the names of tasks relevant to the open program.

Task A personal or work-related activity that you want to keep track of until it is complete.

Task body The blank area in the lower half of the task form in which you can add information not otherwise specified in the form.

Tasks module A component in Outlook that displays and manages your tasks.

Third party Someone to whom you forward a message who was not included in the original email message exchange.

Title bar Displays the name of the program and the program window control buttons—Minimize, Maximize/Restore Down, and Close.

Views Ways to look at similar information in different formats and arrangements.

Wizard A tool that walks you through a process in a step-by-step manner.

Work Week arrangement A calendar arrangement view that shows only the weekdays, Monday through Friday.

Zoom level Displays the Zoom levels on a slider.

OUTLOOK

CHAPTER REVIEW

Apply **1A** skills from these Objectives:

1 Start and Navigate Outlook

2 Send and Receive Email messages

3 Manage Email

Mastering Outlook   Project 1C Enrollment Inbox

In the following project, you will reply to email messages and print your Drafts folder in Table Style. Your completed printout will look similar to the one shown in Figure 1.55.

PROJECT FILES

For Project 1C, you will need the following files:

o01C_Enrollments_Inbox

o01C_Enrollments_Schedule

You will save your file as:

Lastname_Firstname_1C_Email_Replies

PROJECT RESULTS

FIGURE 1.55

(Project 1C Enrollment Inbox continues on the next page)

CHAPTER REVIEW

1 ▶ Log in to the local Windows account that you have set up for the projects in this textbook, and then start Outlook 2013. Click the **FILE tab**, click **Options**, and then in the **Outlook Options** dialog box, on the left, click **Advanced**.

2 ▶ Scroll down to the section **Send and receive**, click to *clear* the check mark from the **Send immediately when connected** check box, and then on the right, click the **Send/Receive** button.

3 ▶ In the **Send/Receive Groups** dialog box, under **Setting for group "All Accounts"**, click to *clear* the **Include this group in send/receive (F9)** check box, and then click to *clear* the **Schedule an automatic send/receive every** check box.

4 ▶ Under **When Outlook is Offline**, click to *clear* the **Include this group in send/receive (F9)** check box.

5 ▶ Click the **Close** button, and then in the **Outlook Options** dialog box, click **OK** to close the dialog box.

6 ▶ On the **Navigation Bar**, click **Mail**. If necessary, delete any items in the **Inbox** folder and the **Drafts** folder.

7 ▶ Click the **FILE tab**, click **Open & Export**, and then click **Import/Export**. In the displayed **Import and Export Wizard** dialog box, under **Choose an action to perform**, click **Import from another program or file**, and then click **Next**.

8 ▶ In the **Import a File** dialog box, under **Select file type to import from**, click **Outlook Data File (.pst)**. Click **Next**. In the **Import Outlook Data File** dialog box, click the **Browse** button. In the **Open Outlook Data Files** dialog box, navigate to the location where the student files for this textbook are stored. Locate **o01C_Enrollments_Inbox**, click one time to select it, and then click **Open**.

9 ▶ Click **Next**, and then click **Finish**. If necessary, on the **Navigation Bar**, click **Mail**, and then in the **Folder Pane**, click **Inbox**. Notice that your **message list** displays two email messages.

10 ▶ In the message list, double-click the *Enrollment Increase* message to open its message window. In the **Respond group**, click **Reply**. With the insertion point positioned above the original message, type **Henry** and then press Enter two times. Type **Yes, I have been hearing about this trend and have some thoughts about it. I can meet with you any day next week. Let me know what time is good for you. I am copying Darron in my reply in**

case he feels he should be involved in our discussion. I am also including a copy of the Winter/Spring schedule. Press Enter two times, and then type **Lisa**

11 ▶ On the **MESSAGE tab**, in the **Include group**, click **Attach File**. In the **Insert File** dialog box, navigate to the student files that accompany this textbook, click **o01C_Enrollments_Schedule**, and then click **Insert**.

12 ▶ In the **Tags group**, mark the message with the **High Importance** tag and set the **Follow Up** flag for **Tomorrow**. In the **Tags group**, click the **Dialog Box Launcher** 🔲, and then set the **Sensitivity** to **Confidential**. **Close** the **Properties** dialog box.

13 ▶ Click **Send**, click **Add Account**, and then click **Cancel** to store the message in your **Drafts** folder. **Close** ☒ the message.

14 ▶ Double-click the *ESL Program Enrollment* message to open its message window, and then **Forward** the message to **HSabaj@LakeMichCityCollege.edu** In the message area, click to position the insertion point above the original message, type **Henry** and then press Enter two times. Type **Regarding the information below from Darron, I think we should discuss this right away**. Press Enter two times, and then type **Lisa**

15 ▶ Click **Send**, click **Add Account**, and then click **Cancel** to store the message in your **Drafts** folder. **Close** ☒ the message.

16 ▶ In the **Folder Pane**, click to select your **Drafts** folder so that your Reply messages display in the **message list**. Click the **FILE tab**, and then click **Print**. Under **Settings**, click **Table Style**. Under **Printer**, click **Print Options**. In the **Print** dialog box, under **Print style**, click **Page Setup**.

17 ▶ In the **Page Setup: Table Style** dialog box, click the **Header/Footer tab**. Under **Footer**, click in the first white box to place the insertion point. Delete any existing text. Using your own first and last name, type **Lastname_Firstname_1C_Email_Replies** Do not be concerned if your text wraps to another line. Delete any existing information in the center and right footer boxes. Under **Header**, if necessary, delete any existing text in the three boxes.

18 ▶ In the **Page Setup: Table Style** dialog box, click the **Paper tab**. Under **Orientation**, click **Portrait** if this option is not already selected. Click **OK** to close the dialog box. At the bottom of the **Print** dialog box, click **Preview**, and notice the footer with your name.

(Project 1C Enrollment Inbox continues on the next page)

CHAPTER REVIEW

19 To print on paper using the printer attached to your system, click the **Print** button. To create an electronic printout, click the **Printer arrow**, click **Microsoft XPS Document Writer**, and then click the **Print** button. In the **Save Print Output As** dialog box, navigate to your **Outlook Chapter 1** folder, and then in the **File name** box, using your own name, type **Lastname_Firstname_1C_Email_Replies**

20 Click **Save**, and then submit this file to your instructor as directed.

21 Delete the contents of the **Inbox** folder, the **Drafts** folder, and the **Deleted Items** folder.

22 Click the **FILE tab**, and then click **Options**. In the **Outlook Options** dialog box, on the left, click **Advanced**. Scroll down as necessary, and then under **Send and receive**, click the **Send immediately when connected** check box. Then, to the right of the check box, click the **Send/Receive** button.

23 In the **Send/Receive Groups** dialog box, under **Setting for group "All Accounts"**, select both the **Include this group in send/receive (F9)** and the **Schedule an automatic send/receive every** check boxes. Under **When Outlook is Offline**, select the check box for **Include this group in send/receive (F9)**. Click **Close** and then click **OK**.

24 Click the **FILE tab**, and then click **Exit**.

END | You have completed Project 1C

CHAPTER REVIEW

Apply **1B** skills from these
Objectives:

4 Create and Edit Contacts

5 Manage Tasks

6 Manage a Calendar

Mastering Outlook | Project 1D Contacts, Tasks, and Appointments

In the following project, you will work with Contacts, Tasks, and Appointments regarding an upcoming Job Fair. Your completed printouts will look similar to those shown in Figure 1.56.

PROJECT FILES

For Project 1D, you will need the following file:

o01D_Job_Fair_Contacts

You will save your files as:

Lastname_Firstname_1D_Contacts_List

Lastname_Firstname_1D_Tasks_List

Lastname_Firstname_1D_Calendar

PROJECT RESULTS

FIGURE 1.56

(Project 1D Contacts, Tasks, and Appointments continues on the next page)

CHAPTER REVIEW

1 Log in to the local Windows account that you have set up for the projects in this textbook, and then start Outlook 2013. If necessary, delete any items from the list of contacts in the People module, and delete any Personal Calendars in the Calendar module.

2 Click the **FILE tab**, click **Open & Export**, and then click **Import/Export**. In the displayed **Import and Export Wizard** dialog box, under **Choose an action to perform**, click **Import from another program or file**, and then click **Next**.

3 In the **Import a File** dialog box, under **Select file type to import from**, click **Outlook Data File (.pst)**. Click **Next**. In the **Import Outlook Data File** dialog box, click the **Browse** button. In the **Open Outlook Data Files** dialog box, navigate to the location where the student files for this textbook are stored. Locate **o01D_Job_Fair_Contacts**, click one time to select it, and then click **Open**.

4 In the **Import Outlook Data File** dialog box, click **Next**, and then click **Finish**.

5 At the bottom of the **Folder Pane**, in the **Navigation Bar**, click **People**. In the **Folder Pane**, be sure your **Contacts** folder is displayed. On the **HOME tab**, in the **New group**, click **New Contact**, and then create a new contact as follows:

> **Jason Moran**
>
> **Park Associates Network Solutions, Inc.**
>
> **JMoran@parkassociates.com**
>
> **626-555-3434**
>
> **333 Rio Grande Ave**
>
> **Desert Park, AZ 95123**

6 On the ribbon of the contact form, on the **CONTACT tab**, in the **Actions group**, click **Save & Close**.

7 Open the contact form for **Laura Wilson-Chavez**, change her **Work** phone number to **805-555-0059** and then click **Save**. **Close** the form.

8 Click the **FILE tab**, click **Print**, and then under **Settings**, click **Phone Directory Style**. Under **Printer**, click **Print Options**. In the **Print** dialog box, click **Page Setup**. In the **Page Setup: Phone Directory Style** dialog box, click the **Header/Footer tab**. Under **Footer**, click in the first white box to place the insertion point. Delete any existing text. Using your own first and last name, type **Lastname_Firstname_1D_Contacts_List** Delete any

existing information in the center and right footer boxes. Under **Header**, if necessary, delete any existing text in the three boxes.

9 In the **Page Setup: Phone Directory Style** dialog box, click the **Paper tab**. Under **Orientation**, click **Portrait** if this option is not already selected. Click **OK**. At the bottom of the **Print** dialog box, click **Preview**, and notice the footer with your name. To print on paper using the printer attached to your system, click the **Print** button. To create an electronic printout, click the **Printer arrow**, click **Microsoft XPS Document Writer**, and then click the **Print** button. In the **Save Print Output As** dialog box, navigate to your **Outlook Chapter 1** folder that you created in Project 1A, and then in the **File name** box, using your own name, type **Lastname_Firstname_1D_Contacts_List** Click **Save**.

10 In the **Navigation Bar**, click **Tasks**. On the ribbon, on the **HOME tab**, in the **New group**, click **New Task**. Create the new task with the subject **Finalize exhibitor list** and with a **Due Date** of two business days from today's date. Change the **Priority** to **High**, and then click **Save & Close**.

11 Add another new task with the subject **Contact rental company regarding setup** Change the **Due Date** to three weeks from today. Add a third task with the subject **Write press release for job fair** Change the **Due Date** to tomorrow, and set the **Priority** to **High**.

12 Click the **FILE tab**, and then click **Print**. Under **Settings**, click **Table Style**. Under **Printer**, click **Print Options**. In the **Print** dialog box, to the right of **Print style**, click **Page Setup**. In the **Page Setup: Table Style** dialog box, click the **Header/Footer tab**. Under **Footer**, click in the first white box to place the insertion point. Delete any existing text. Using your own first and last name, type **Lastname_Firstname_1D_Tasks_List** Do not be concerned if your text wraps to another line. Delete any existing information in the center and right footer boxes. Under **Header**, if necessary, delete any existing text in the three boxes.

13 In the **Page Setup: Table Style** dialog box, click the **Paper tab**. Under **Orientation**, click **Portrait** if this option is not already selected. Click **OK**. At the bottom of the **Print** dialog box, click **Preview**, and notice the footer with your name.

(Project 1D Contacts, Tasks, and Appointments continues on the next page)

CHAPTER REVIEW

14 To print on paper using the printer attached to your system, click the **Print** button. To create an electronic printout, click the **Printer arrow**, click **Microsoft XPS Document Writer**, and then click the **Print** button. In the **Save Print Output As** dialog box, navigate to your **Outlook Chapter 1** folder, and then in the **File name** box, using your own name, type **Lastname_Firstname_1D_Tasks_List** and click **Save**.

15 On the **Navigation Bar**, click **Calendar**. On the ribbon, click the **FOLDER tab**. In the **New group**, click **New Calendar**. In the displayed **Create New Folder** dialog box, in the **Name** box, type **Personal Calendar** and then click **OK**.

16 In the **Folder Pane**, under **My Calendars**, click the **Personal Calendar** check box. In the **Folder Pane**, click to clear the **Calendar** check box to display only the Personal Calendar.

17 In the **Date Navigator**, click the **right arrow** one time, advancing the calendar to the next month. Click the **Monday** of the first full week of the displayed month. On the **VIEW tab**, set the **Arrangement** to **Week**. Then click the **HOME tab**. In the first full week of the displayed month, create the following appointments by clicking **New Appointment** in the **New group**:

Monday: As the **Subject** type **Meet with Bradley to discuss Job Fair refreshments** As the **Location** type **Bradley's office** If necessary, clear the **All day event** check box, and then set the **Start time** to **10:00 AM** and **End time** to **11:00 AM**.

Tuesday: As the **Subject** type **Meet with Jane Houston** As the **Location** type **My office** If necessary, clear the **All day event** check box, and then set the **Start time** to **1:00 PM** and **End time** to **1:30 PM**.

Thursday: As the **Subject** type **Pre-Fair Staff Meeting** As the **Location** type **West Conference Room** Set the **Start time** to **9:00 AM** and the **End time** to **11:00 AM**.

18 Click the **FILE tab**, click **Print**, and then under **Settings**, click **Weekly Agenda Style**. Under **Printer**, click

Print Options. In the **Print** dialog box, under **Print style**, click **Page Setup**.

19 In the **Page Setup: Weekly Agenda Style** dialog box, click the **Header/Footer tab**. Under **Footer**, click in the first white box to place the insertion point. Delete any existing text. Using your own first and last name, type **Lastname_Firstname_1D_Calendar** Do not be concerned if your text wraps to another line. Delete any existing information in the center and right footer boxes. Under **Header**, if necessary, delete any existing text in the three boxes.

20 In the **Page Setup: Weekly Agenda Style** dialog box, click the **Paper tab**. Under **Orientation**, click **Portrait** if this option is not already selected. Click **OK**. At the bottom of the **Print** dialog box, click **Preview**, and notice the footer with your name.

21 To print on paper using the printer attached to your system, click the **Print** button. To create an electronic printout, click the **Printer arrow**, click **Microsoft XPS Document Writer**, and then click the **Print** button. In the **Save Print Output As** dialog box, navigate to your **Outlook Chapter 1** folder, and then in the **File name** box, using your own name, type **Lastname_Firstname_1D_Calendar** Click **Save**.

22 Just above the **Navigation Bar**, point to **Personal Calendar**—be sure you are pointing to **Personal Calendar**—right-click to display a shortcut menu, and then click **Delete Calendar**. When the message *Move "Personal Calendar" to your Deleted Items folder* displays, click **Yes**.

23 On the **Navigation Bar**, click **People**. Press Ctrl + A to select all the Contacts, and then press Delete. On the **Navigation Bar**, click **Mail**, press Ctrl + A to select all items, and then press Delete, and then click **Yes**. Right-click the **Deleted Items** folder, and click **Empty Folder**, and then click **Yes**.

24 **Close** Outlook. Submit the three files that are the results of this project to your instructor as directed.

END | You have completed Project 1D

OUTCOMES-BASED ASSESSMENTS

Apply a combination of the **1A** and **1B** skills.

GO! Think   Project 1E Youth Softball

PROJECT FILES

For Project 1E, you will need the following file:

New blank Appointment form

You will save your document as:

Lastname_Firstname_1E_Softball_Calendar

Jameson Taylor, the Information Technology Director for the City of Desert Park, is an avid softball player, and he also coaches the city's youth softball team. At the end of every season, the city hosts a barbeque for the team members. This year, the team has made the playoffs. You will manage Mr. Taylor's calendar for the week of the playoffs and the barbeque, creating appointments for the practices, games, and barbeque.

Log in to the Windows account you are using for this chapter, and then start Outlook. In the Calendar, display the first full week of May to create Mr. Taylor's schedule for the week. Create a new appointment for Tuesday for softball practice from 5:30 to 7:30 p.m. with no reminders. Create an hour-long appointment on Wednesday morning with the team's assistant coach, and use a playoff-related subject. Create an appointment on Wednesday with the subject *Your softball practice* from 3:30 to 5:30 p.m.

On Thursday of that same week, create an appointment for Playoffs from 3:30 to 6:00 p.m. On Thursday morning, create an hour-long appointment with city catering vendor with a subject related to the barbeque. On Friday, create a new appointment for the barbeque from 6:00 to 8:00 p.m.

Print the week's appointments using the Weekly Agenda Style. Add the footer **Lastname_Firstname_1E_Softball_Calendar** To create an electronic printout, click the Printer arrow, click Microsoft XPS Document Writer, and then click the Print button. In the Save Print Output As dialog box, navigate to your **Outlook Chapter 1** folder, and then in the File name box, using your own name, type **Lastname_Firstname_1E_Softball_Calendar** Click Save.

Delete all the calendar entries, close Outlook, and then submit the file to your instructor as directed.

END | You have completed Project 1E

Index

A

accounts, 3–5. *See also* email accounts
Add Account dialog box, 12, 17–19, 21, 23
administrator account, 4
appointment area, 38–41, 46
appointments
    defined, 38, 46
    scheduling, 40–42
at sign (@), 9, 46
Attachment column heading, 24–25
attachments, 15–16, 18–19, 46
AutoComplete, 18, 22, 46

B

Backstage view, 7, 9, 46
body, of task, 37, 47
business days, 36, 44, 46

C

calendars, 38–43
Calendar module, 7–8, 44, 46
Calendar peek, 38, 46
Cancel Email Account Setup dialog box, 5
carbon copy (Cc), 11, 46
charms, 3
Close, window control button, 7, 47
closing email messages, 14–15
column headings, 23–25, 46
components, Outlook, 3. *See also* modules
computers, Microsoft account and, 3
configuring Outlook, for email messages,
    9–10
contact list, 34–36
contacts
    creating, 32–34
    defined, 3, 31, 46
    importing, into People module, 31
    Notes area, 32, 46
    People Card, 31, 34, 46
    People module, 8, 31, 44, 46
    as personal information manager, 1, 3,
        44, 46
control buttons, window, 7, 47
conversations, 25, 46
courtesy copy (Cc), 11, 46
Create New Folder dialog box, 39
Ctrl + End, 12
Ctrl + Home, 12
Ctrl + O, 15, 34
Custom dialog box, 21

D

Data File. *See* Outlook Data File
Date Navigator, 38–40, 42, 46
days, business, 36, 44, 46
deleting messages, 28–29

delivery options, message, 23, 46
dialog boxes. *See specific dialog boxes*
dictionary, Word's, 12
domain name, 9, 11, 46
drafts, 12
Drafts folder, 2, 12, 17–19, 21, 23, 27–28
dragging, 3, 18, 47

E

editing contact list, 34–36
editors, email, 10
email accounts
    Outlook Data File for, 44
    Outlook Today and, 6, 46
    profile, 5–6, 46
email addresses
    AutoComplete, 18, 22, 46
    components of, 9
    domain name, 9, 11, 46
    flagging, 20–21, 46
    at sign (@), 9, 46
    syntax, 11, 47
    underlined, 11
email editors, 10
email messages. *See also* Inbox
    Attachment column heading, 24–25
    attachments, 15–16, 18–19, 46
    Cc, 11, 46
    closing, 14–15
    configuring Outlook for, 9–10
    conversations, 25, 46
    creating, 10–12
    deleting, 28–29
    delivery options, 23, 46
    Drafts folder, 2, 12, 17–19, 21, 23, 27–28
    etiquette, 11, 44
    fields, 23–24, 46
    formatting text, 20–21, 46
    forwarding, 17–18, 46, 47
    frequent usage of, 44
    FW prefix, 17–18
    header, 14–15, 46
    importance label, 20, 23, 46
    importing, to Inbox, 13–14
    marking, 20–21
    message list, 7, 14–16, 18, 20–21, 23, 25,
        27–28, 36, 46
    navigating, 14–15
    opening, 14–16
    printing, 25–27
    RE prefix, 16–18, 46
    replying to, 16–17
    sending, 10–12, 18–19
    sensitivity label, 20, 23, 47
    settings, 23
    sorting, Inbox, 23–25
    third party, 17, 47
    unread, 14–15, 20

End, keystroke, 12
etiquette, email, 11, 44
exploring Calendar, 38–40
exploring Outlook, 6–9

F

fields, message, 23–24, 46
file management, Backstage view, 7, 9, 46
FILE tab, 6–7, 46
flagging, 20–21, 46
Folder Pane, 6–7, 46
folders. *See also* Inbox; modules
    Drafts, 2, 12, 17–19, 21, 23, 27–28
    for modules, 44
    Outlook's components in, 3
    personal information in, 3, 25, 44
footers. *See* headers and footers
formatting text, 20–21, 46
forwarding email messages, 17–18, 46, 47
FW prefix, 17–18

G

gestures, touchscreen, 3
grammar and spelling checker, 22
Group names, 6–7, 46

H

header, message, 14–15, 46
headers and footers, 27, 35
Help button, 6–7, 29, 46
Help feature, Outlook, 29
high resolution, 7, 47
Home, keystroke, 12
host name, domain name, 9, 11, 46

I

Import a File dialog box, 13, 41
Import and Export Wizard dialog box,
    13, 31
Import Outlook Data File dialog box, 13, 31
importance label, messages, 20, 23, 46
importing
    contacts, into People module, 31
    defined, 46
    messages, to Inbox, 13–14
Inbox
    defined, 3, 46
    importing messages to, 13–14
    sorting messages, 23–25
Insert File dialog box, 19
insertion point, keystrokes for, 12

K

keyboard shortcut, Ctrl + O, 15, 34
keystrokes, for moving insertion
    point, 12

L

left mouse button, 33, 36
local user account, 3–5
Location Information dialog box, 32

M

Mail module, 7, 14, 44, 46
marking messages, 20–21
Maximize, 7, 47
Memo Style, 25, 27, 46
message header, 14–15, 46
message list, 7, 14–16, 18, 20–21, 23, 25, 27–28, 36, 46
messages. *See* email messages
Microsoft account, 3
Microsoft Office Outlook 2013. *See* Outlook 2013
Microsoft Outlook dialog box, 29
Microsoft Word dictionary, 12
Microsoft Word editor, 10
Minimize, 7, 47
modules, Outlook
  benefits of, 44
  Calendar, 7–8, 44, 46
  Folder pane, 6–7, 46
  folders for, 44
  Mail, 7, 14, 44, 46
  People, 8, 31, 44, 46
  Tasks, 8–9, 36, 44, 47
  views, 3, 7, 46, 47
mouse
  dragging, 3, 18, 47
  left mouse button, 33, 36
move up/down one line, 12
moving insertion point, keystrokes for, 12
multiple computers, Microsoft account, 3
multiple recipients, replying to, 17

N

navigating messages, 14–15
Navigation Bar, 6–7, 46
Navigator, Date, 38–40, 42, 46
Notes area, contacts, 32, 46

O

offline, 9–10, 29, 46
online, 9, 46
Open Outlook Data Files dialog box, 13, 31
opening messages, 14–16
Outlook 2013 (Microsoft Office Outlook 2013)
  configuring, for email messages, 9–10
  exploring, 6–9
  functions of, 1, 3, 44
  as personal information manager, 1, 3, 44, 46
  screen elements, 6–7
Outlook Data File (.pst), 13, 31, 44
Outlook editor, 10
Outlook Help feature, 29

Outlook modules. *See* modules
Outlook Options dialog box, 9–10, 29
Outlook Today, 6, 46

P

Page Setup: Phone Directory Style dialog box, 36
Page Setup: Table Style dialog box, 26–27, 35, 37
Page Setup: Weekly Agenda Style dialog box, 42
Page Setup dialog box, 27, 35
PageUp, 12
password, 4–6
People Card, 31, 34, 46
People module, 8, 31, 44, 46
personal information, in folders, 3, 25, 44
personal information manager, 1, 3, 44, 46
PgDn, 12
pinch, stretch and, 3
prefix FW, 17–18
prefix RE, 16–18, 46
press and hold, touchscreen gesture, 3
Print dialog box, 26–27, 35–38, 42
print styles
  defined, 25, 46
  Memo Style, 25, 27, 46
  Table Style, 25–27, 35, 37, 47
printing
  calendars, 42–43
  contact list, 34–36
  email messages, 25–27
  to-do list, 36–38
profile, 5–6, 46
Properties dialog box, 23
Protected View, 16
.pst. *See* Outlook Data File

Q

Quick Access Toolbar, 6–7, 14–15, 46

R

RE prefix, 16–18, 46
Reader app, 27
Reading Pane, 7, 14–17, 21, 23–25, 46
recipients, replying to, 17
red wavy line, 12, 22
Reply All button, 17
replying, to email messages, 16–17
resolution, screen, 7, 47
Restore Down, 7, 47
ribbon
  with commands, 10–11
  description, 6–7, 46–47
right-click, press and hold, 3

S

Save Print Output As dialog box, 27, 36, 38, 42
scheduling appointments, 40–42
screen elements, Outlook, 6–7

screen resolution, 7, 47
security label, sensitivity, 20, 23, 47
selecting text, 18, 47
sending email messages, 10–12, 18–19
Send/Receive Groups dialog box, 10, 29
sensitivity label, 20, 23, 47
settings, email, 23
shortcut menu, 15, 20, 22, 28, 43
Sign in without a Microsoft account option, 4
slide, touchscreen gesture, 3
slider, Zoom level, 6–7, 47
sorting Inbox messages, 23–25
spelling and grammar checker, 22
Start screen, Windows 8, 4–5
stretch, pinch and, 3
swipe, touchscreen gesture, 3
syntax, message, 11, 47

T

Table Style, 25–27, 35, 37, 47
tabs, 7, 46, 47. *See also specific tabs*
tap, touchscreen gesture, 3
tasks, 36–38, 47
task body, 37, 47
task-oriented tabs, 7, 46
Tasks module, 8–9, 36, 44, 47
text
  formatting, 20–21, 46
  selecting, 18, 47
third party, 17, 47
Title bar, 6–7, 47
to-do list, 36–38
touchscreen gestures, 3

U

underlined email addresses, 11
unread messages, 14–15, 20
user account, local, 5–7

V

views, 3, 7, 46, 47. *See also* modules

W

wavy red line, 12, 22
Week, Work, 39, 47
window control buttons, 7, 47
Windows 8
  local user account, 5–7
  Microsoft account, 3
  Reader app, 27
  start screen, 4–5
  touchscreen gestures, 3
Windows Store, 3
wizard, 13, 31, 47
Work Week, 39, 47

Z

zoom, pinch/stretch, 3
Zoom level, 6–7, 47